FIELD
of HOPE

◆ AN INSPIRING AUTOBIOGRAPHY OF ◆
A LIFETIME OF OVERCOMING ODDS

FIELD
of HOPE

◆ AN INSPIRING AUTOBIOGRAPHY OF ◆
A LIFETIME OF OVERCOMING ODDS

BRETT BUTLER
with JERRY B. JENKINS

THOMAS NELSON PUBLISHERS
Nashville * Atlanta * London * Vancouver
Printed in the United States of America

To my wife Eveline,
my loving children,
my close friends,
and those who prayed for me—
you share in our miracle

Published in Nashville, Tennessee, by Thomas Nelson, Inc., Publishers, and distributed in Canada by Word Communications, Ltd., Richmond, British Columbia.

The Bible version used in this publication is THE NEW KING JAMES VERSION. Copyright © 1979, 1980, 1982, 1990, Thomas Nelson, Inc., Publishers.

ISBN 0-7852-7144-9

Printed in the United States of America.

1   2   3   4   5   6   BVG   02   01   00   99   98   97

◆ ACKNOWLEDGMENTS ◆

Special thanks to Derrick Hall of the
Dodgers, Rennie Rees and Shannon
Kurtz in Jerry Jenkins's office,
and to the many who graciously agreed
to interviews

◆ CONTENTS ◆

PROVING PEOPLE WRONG

I'm not a complicated guy.

With me the cliché is true: What you see is what you get. I care what people think about me. You will always know where you stand. I wear my emotions on my sleeve.

If I'm smiling, I'm happy. If my grin is impish, I've likely just pulled some prank. If I'm squinting, I'm concentrating. If I'm scowling, I'm not happy. It's as simple as that.

People tell me I don't look my age. Only a streak of gray hair right in front hints that I'm one who has cheated Father Time. Unless something has happened between the writing and the publishing of this book, I'm the oldest starting outfielder and lead-off man in baseball. My colleagues and I are all grown men playing a boys' game, but I'm old enough to be the father of some of them.

That, ironically, is because my weakness has become my strength. For years being small and light was the obstacle I had to overcome to stay in the game. Now it's what still allows me to play like a young man. I can take the ribbing for having the "smallest feet'' in the majors. Nearly every other player who came up when I did is now on the banquet circuit. I'm on a pennant-contender.

I'm not bragging. I've lived every American boy's dream, and I'm grateful. Because of my size I had to believe in myself when no one else did, to show that confidence when the decision-makers were watching, and to prove myself over and over through the years. I admit it: I carried myself, especially early on, with the swagger of the cocky upstart. To me it was a means to an end. I had to stand out to be noticed. I wasn't afraid of confrontation. My yes was yes and my no was no.

I have strong opinions and I'm not hesitant to air them. The truth is, I'd rather my life and my performance on the field do my talking for me. But sometimes things happen in a person's life that just have to be told. Before a little more than a year ago I would not have been interested in writing a book, especially about my life. Now, though, I have so much to tell, I can't keep quiet. Because of what happened, I'm forced to appear to be writing about myself, but you're going to see that this is not really about me. This is about my life, my wife, my kids, my friends, and the thousands of people who prayed for me. The fiber and character of my being will be revealed in this book—the adversities, the trials, the overcoming, the proving people wrong.

I was the ''lucky'' one, the one who seemed to be put down. But all that did was show me what I really had in this life, and believe me, it proved to be so much more than the privileges of a professional baseball player.

My story is first about my parents. Like anyone else, I was shaped by my upbringing. Then it's about Eveline, my rock. When we met and fell in love it might have been said that I was rescuing her from a difficult past. Yet in the hour of my greatest need, she had to be stronger for me than I ever had to be for her. My story is also about family and friends that make a man wealthy beyond his imagination.

And finally, my story is about God. I'm thankful he's the God of second chances and new beginnings. I've been given more than my share, and I can't wait to tell you about it.

Brett Butler
Los Angeles
May 1997

WHEN IT RAINS, IT POURS

I looked forward to spring training with the Dodgers in 1996. The last year or so had been tough. Having been embroiled in the baseball strike, feeling jilted by Los Angeles before signing with New York as a free agent, losing my beloved mother to cancer, and being traded from the Mets back to the Dodgers only to find myself in the middle of yet another controversy, I was ready for one last season.

I would turn thirty-nine in June and believed the Dodgers had a chance to win the World Series. That would be the perfect way to finish what I had always considered a storybook career.

Two weeks before leaving for spring training, I felt a tickle in my throat. The next day it was sore and kept bothering me. Finally I went to my friend Bob Gadlage, an ear, nose, and throat specialist. He examined me and said I had tonsillitis, "a kid's disease." I decided to worry about it later.

I went to spring training with my family's blessing. Well, most of my family's blessing, anyway. For the last four or five years we've taken it to a family vote. Do you want Dad to play or not? Yes or no? Everybody wanted me to play, except Blake, the youngest of our four children and our only son. He wants me around more. That works on me, and it won't be long before he'll have more of me than he can handle.

I had a great spring. I started fast and hit about .390. Except for that nagging sore throat and a little more fatigue than usual, I felt great. I attributed my tiredness to age and wondered if I would have to do something about my tonsils if the medication didn't clear them up. Some days I had more trouble swallowing than others. I prayed that a tune-up in my dosages would allow me to forget about my throat and concentrate on baseball.

Despite how well I hit in spring training, my throat bothered me more every day. I was sleeping longer. I've always liked my sleep, but I really needed it now.

Bob Gadlage had given me steroids and antibiotics that he thought would knock out my infection in a couple of weeks. When two weeks went by and it wasn't gone, Mickey Mellman, our team physician, prescribed stronger antibiotics. A week later, he prescribed more.

Dr. Gadlage, a big Braves fan, came to spring training and made it a point to come over and see me. He looked in my throat toward the end of spring training. "Your tonsils are slightly bigger, but not that bad," he said. "We can do a little more with antibiotics, but you're going to have to get these taken out."

I said, "Can it wait till the end of the year?"

"Yeah, that would probably be fine. Unless the tonsillitis gets worse. Then it will be your call."

I started the season fairly well, hitting about .300. At the end of April, Eveline looked at my throat. "There's something wrong, Brett. You need to come home to Atlanta with me."

"Eveline," I said, "Eric (Karros) is hurt, Greg (Gagne) is hurt. I can't leave now. Maybe I'll have a tonsillectomy over the All-Star break, but I'm not doing it now."

"I just think something's wrong," she repeated.

I knew she was right, but I hoped the problem would take care of itself. I knew it could take as long as a month to recover from a tonsillectomy, and I wanted to put it off as long as possible. Some of the new medication reduced the swelling, but people had been noticing a lump on the right side of my throat as early as March. By the time Eveline begged me to come home with her, I felt the antibiotics were sapping my strength and affecting my performance.

Eveline, who has always been into holistic and alternative medicine, was direct with the Dodger trainers, telling them I was going to get off antibiotics. My dosages and types of antibiotics had been changed so many times that the treatment was counterproductive.

Tommy Lasorda called me into his office. "How do you feel, Brett?"

"I'm a little worn down, Skip. A little tired. My throat still hurts from this tonsil."

"The reason I'm asking is that I'm thinking about giving you a couple of days off."

Immediately it hit me that he was saying this not because I was sick but because my average had dropped to .265, and I was looking tired and weak. *He thinks I'm too old and can't do this anymore,* I thought.

"You know, Tommy, the more I think about it, if you're going to give me a couple of days off, what I ought to do is call my surgeon and get my tonsils out. I'll probably be out four or five weeks, but then I'll still have several months left, and I'll be fine. The way I'm feeling right now, I'm just not going to be able to play up to the level I want to."

"Do what you think is best, Brett. We'll do whatever you say."

I met with Tommy, Dodgers general manager Fred Claire, and the trainers, and we decided I would play the next two days. The following day, a Thursday, would be a day off anyway. I would use that day to fly home, then have my tonsils out on Friday.

In my final at bat of that second game, I singled home a run.

That felt good. I looked forward to getting relief from my sore throat and getting back to baseball. Before I left I sought out Roger Cedeno, the rookie who would fill in for me. "Roger," I said, "I'll be gone several weeks. Here's your chance to play every day and take my job."

Later he would be very generous talking about how much it meant to him that I was free with advice and encouragement.

Two days later Eveline and I were met at the hospital by our friends Lowery and Vicki Robinson and Tim Cash, a former baseball player now in the ministry. They would be the first of several friends who would stand by us with love and support. At that point, of course, none of us realized how serious the situation was. This was still funny to all of us: a grown man with a child's disease, getting his tonsils out.

We were giddy. We didn't know Dr. Gadlage had awakened at three o'clock in the morning that day, troubled over my surgery. He had done hundreds of these, and had never had trouble sleeping.

Eveline takes up the story here, because when I was wheeled in for the pre-operative exam, I was already doped up enough to be out of it:

This was to be same-day surgery. I brought Brett in and I would take him home when it was over. Everything had been done except the operation. I had signed all the papers, Brett had been prepped, and now Bob Gadlage was going to take one last look before surgery.

We were all pretty upbeat. I was excited about getting this over with so Brett could start feeling better and get back to baseball. Lowery and Tim were cutting up as usual, right at the edge of getting kicked out of the hospital for having too much fun. When Dr. Bob came in, I said, "So, Bob, how long is this gonna take?"

He said, "Why? Do you have somewhere you need to be?"

"Yeah! We're starving. We want to go have some breakfast."

"Well," he said, "it will take me about forty-five minutes. An hour if I decide to take a nap."

Lowery and Vicki and Tim and I were chitchatting when Bob said, "Let's have a look at this patient and see how we're doing."

He opened Brett's mouth and peered in, then recoiled and stepped back. He bumped into me. I had my back to him and didn't know what was happening. He said somberly, "Eveline, I'll see you after the surgery."

I said, "Oh, what? Now you're going to be Mr. Doctor, so you have to be all serious on me?"

He didn't smile. "I'll come back and talk to you as soon as we're through."

As Brett was being wheeled out, Lowery said to Tim, "Did you see the look on his face when he looked in Brett's mouth? He looked shocked."

The four of us went into the waiting room and prayed for Brett. Tim went off to go to the bathroom and Lowery followed him, up to no good. Once Tim was in there, Lowery jiggled the door handle and we could hear Tim hollering, "Hey! Hey! There's someone in here!" Vicki and I laughed our heads off. Then Tim figured out it was Lowery, and kept saying, "Lowery, cut it out! Cut it out!"

Tim was still in there when Lowery came back and we saw a little old man with a cane shuffling toward the bathroom. We started giggling, knowing that he was going to try that door. Sure enough, he did. We could hear Tim from down the hall, "You'd better get out of here!" The man nearly fell over, and we laughed so hard we almost slipped off our chairs. I was convinced those guys were going to get us kicked out of the hospital.

Forty-five minutes later, when the tonsillectomy should have been over, we were still cutting up and trying to keep from laughing too loud. Then it was an hour, and someone joked that Dr. Bob must have taken a nap. When an hour and fifteen minutes had passed, we were starting to get quiet. I kept looking at my watch, walking out of the room, looking down the hallway, walking back in, and walking back out.

Vicki said, "Are you getting nervous?"

"Well, either there's a problem or Bob's taking an awfully long nap," I said.

I decided to sit still until the one-hour-and-forty-five-minute mark. When that came, I walked out and peeked down the hallway. There came Bob out the door. I poked my head into the waiting room. "Here he comes!"

I met Bob down the hall and he said, "First, I want you to know that Brett's okay."

"Well, of course he is."

"I haven't taken his tonsils out yet."

"Why not?"

"I had to call in an oncologist."

"And why would you do that?" By now my friends had joined me.

"Eveline, I hadn't seen Brett since spring training. His right tonsil is three times bigger than when I saw him just a few weeks ago. We've done a biopsy and have taken it to pathology."

"What are you telling me, Bob?"

"At this point, we don't know."

Tim, our huge friend, put his arm around me. I looked up at him and looked back at Bob, and for one of the very few times in my life, I heard the Lord speak clearly to me in my mind. He said, *Do you trust me? Do you trust me?* I silently said yes.

Bob said, "What I'd like to do is wake Brett up, do an MRI, and see exactly what we're dealing with."

I responded immediately, "Absolutely not. You get in there and you take that thing out. If you have to tell Brett he has cancer, then you tell him later. But you're not going to wake him, tell him he might have cancer, and then do an MRI besides what you're going to do later. Let's just get that thing out of him."

Bob agreed, but he said, "Eveline, I'm not an oncologist. I've got one coming in to assist me, one of the best. He knows what he's doing. We're on the phone to Emory University right now talking to them about the best way to remove it."

The question was whether to go in through Brett's mouth or in through the side of his neck. Bob told me they would be dangerously close to Brett's carotid artery. "If that ruptures, it may be very difficult to stop the bleeding, and you need to know that going in."

"Bob, I trust you, and I trust God. So you go do whatever you have to do."

I didn't really need to ask any questions. I knew Brett had cancer. I knew it because God had asked me if I trusted him.

Bob said the surgery would take a couple of hours. He and the other physician, Dr. Samuel Hanovar, dislocated Brett's jaw and carefully removed both tonsils. The right one contained a plum-sized tumor they immediately sent for evaluation. Until we heard something definite, I didn't want to call any of our friends. I told Vicki and Lowery and Tim not to tell anybody. I would call our tightest circle of friends—Steve and Indy Cesari and Steve and Suzanne Dils—but certainly not the press.

I did call Mackie Shilstone, the friend who is a sports performance expert from New Orleans and who knew all of Brett's medical history since they had met in San Francisco. Brett went to him every year to work out and stay in shape. I told Mackie to check Brett's most recent blood tests at the Kenner Regional Medical Center. If this was cancer, I wanted to know how long he had had it. If it had been in his system for a year, it should have been in the blood tests done at Kenner in December.

When Dr. Bob came out of surgery the second time, he was starting to tell me how things went when the other doctor called him back in, saying, "Come here! I've never seen anything like this before!"

Bob apologized later for that less-than-professional announcement, but he was also encouraged that "this thing doesn't cut like cancer, feel like cancer, or look like cancer."

I knew in my heart it was cancer. I just knew.

Bob took us all into the doctor's lounge where Lowery and Tim started asking a lot of questions I wouldn't have thought of.

I insisted on being with Brett when Bob told him what was going on. Our three friends wanted to be there, too, so we all crowded into the room.

Bob told Brett the whole story, and I saw God's hand in it from the beginning. First, Bob usually does this surgery at his own office. Had he done that, he would have had to wait longer for the oncologist, who just happened to be heading toward the hospital when Bob needed him. Bob also confirmed that he had indeed been shocked when he saw how quickly the tonsil had grown since he'd seen it last. He was still trying to remain optimistic, because of the unusual nature of the lump. I could tell from the looks on the faces of the oncologist and the anesthesiologist that they would confirm my worst fears. But Bob told us not to jump to any conclusions until they had hard data. He told me to take Brett home, that he would drop in on him Saturday, and that he would have the test results by Monday.

I had to decide how I was going to respond to the many friends and loved ones who would call to see how he came through his tonsillectomy. I'm a terrible liar. People can see right through me. Brett was taking the high road, believing this was anything but cancer. Still, he was in total misery. His throat hurt so bad he couldn't swallow. He couldn't sleep.

I got a call from Tim Brown, a writer for the *Daily News*. He had met Brett in spring training and they had somehow immediately hit it off. He asked, "How's Brett doing?"

"As well as can be expected."

"There weren't any complications?"

"None that we know of."

Brett liked and trusted Tim so much that he would be the first member of the press we would tell, when there was something to say.

Only Steve and Indy, Lowery and Vicki, and Steve and Suzanne knew the possibilities. Everyone else thought Brett had a simple tonsillectomy. Our friends were wonderful. They were bringing meals, flowers, notes, whatever they thought would cheer him up.

The hardest phone call for me was from Brett's sister, Bev. If for some reason this wasn't cancer, I certainly didn't want to bring back all those feelings she would have had when their mother died. This was her big brother, and they're real close. She thinks the world of him. It was difficult not to tell Bev that Brett might have cancer, but I knew it would have crushed her.

Dr. Bob dropped by on Saturday just to check on Brett. He said he would call with some sort of confirmation of the test results on Monday, because, "I'm going to be in surgery all day and I won't have a chance to get over here. I'll call to let you know what's going on."

By Sunday, Brett still had no relief. He was in agony. Every time he wanted to swallow he had to get in a certain position, grit his teeth, clench his fists, and hunch over. About the only thing he could ingest were ice shavings, letting them melt and then carefully letting the cool water trickle down his throat. More than once he said, "Eveline, just shoot me."

He wasn't seriously suicidal, of course, but I got the picture. This was a pain worse than death.

Monday afternoon I was making phone calls at Brett's desk, which faces the courtyard in front of our house. It was a bright, sunshiny day. I was in the middle of a conversation when Bob drove in. That brought me up short. He had said he would be in surgery all day and would just call us with the test results. Now here he was. That could only mean bad news.

Bob is a close friend and normally just walks in our house and finds Brett. But now he came in the front door and just stood in the entryway. I heard Brett get up and start heading our way. I quickly got off the phone and joined them. Bob said, "How are you feeling?"

"If you're here, it must be bad news," Brett said.

"Let me just check you out." I noticed Bob wasn't touching Brett's throat. He was feeling the back of his neck, up and down. Bob said, "Let's sit down."

"That doesn't sound so good," I said.

Brett and I sat on the sofa. Bob remained standing. "We got the pathology report today," he said. "All twelve pathologists at DeKalb Medical confirmed that this is squamous cell carcinoma. It is cancer."

I just sat there with a blank stare. Eveline says I ran my hand through my hair. Bob said, "Brett, I just want to tell you that you're going to die one day, but it isn't going to be from this."

"I hope you can back that up," Eveline said.

I was stunned. I didn't know anything could be worse than the pain I felt in my throat just then, but suddenly the future appeared before me and it didn't look bright. That instant the sky literally turned black and hailstones began dropping all over our yard. Eveline said, "God must really be angry right now."

She believed, along with my young teammate, Todd Hollandsworth, that Satan was trying to take one of God's elect. God doesn't bring bad things upon us, Satan does.

I had never seen such an immediate change in the weather. It went from bright sun to black as night and started hailing. Bob still talks about how eerie it was to pull into our driveway in sunlight and see the sun disappear while he was giving us the worst news of our lives.

Eveline said, "Bob, would you tell the kids? Would you explain exactly what Brett has? I want them to know what's going to happen from here, and I'd appreciate it if you'd answer their questions."

Bob says our beautiful children are like "Precious Moments dolls." He's always found them beyond their years in wisdom and understanding. Yet this had to be a difficult chore. We called the kids into the den, and Bob explained from the beginning. "We took your daddy's tonsil out, and we found something inside it. Your dad has cancer . . ."

All four kids began crying. Blake asked, "Is Daddy gonna die like Grandma?"

"No," Bob said. "Your grandma had a very bad cancer. She had lung cancer and then she had brain cancer, and those are very bad. There's nothing they could really do for your grandma. But there's a lot we can do for your dad. There's a better chance that your dad's going to live than that he's going to die."

It had to be awful for the kids. They had seen their grandmother become someone they didn't even recognize. That's what they related to cancer. They also wanted to know if it hurt. I was glad to hear the tonsil surgery would be more painful than whatever cancer surgery had to be performed. I couldn't imagine anything worse than what I was already suffering.

When Bob finally left, the sky cleared and the sun reappeared. It was the strangest thing I had ever seen.

Now it was time to tell our friends and family. That difficult task fell to Eveline.

She recalls: "I couldn't reach Lowery, so I called Vicki. She cried over the phone. I called Steve and Indy and told them, and we cried some more. Everybody I called wound up crying, and so did I. Finally I decided I couldn't cry anymore. I had to be strong. I couldn't just sit and boo-hoo every time I talked to someone. Dr. Gadlage had only been gone about half an hour when I heard insistent knocking and the doorbell ringing. I hurried to the door thinking, *Good grief!* When I opened it, there stood Lowery. He could barely speak. He just grabbed me and started crying.

"It was hard for Lowery because he lost both his parents when he was young and he's always been on his own. He has no siblings except for a couple of stepsisters much older than he is. He's always felt Brett and I are his only family. Now, it was like he had cancer too. He rushed to Brett and just sat there. They cried and prayed together. I left the room. I couldn't handle that. It would have crushed me to see the two of them, best buddies, willing to die for each other.

"Brett couldn't face calling Beverly, and that was the call I dreaded the most too. When she answered the phone, I said, 'Bev, is Paul there? Let me talk to him for a second.'

" 'Paul, I'm about to tell Beverly something very devastating,' I said. 'Brett has cancer.'

" 'What!?' "

" 'With everything else Bev's been through with her mother, she's going to need your support. Just be ready to put your arms around her and comfort her through this. . . . Now let me talk to her.'

"Bev came on the phone. 'What's going on?'

"I said, 'Beverly, I just told Paul that you're really going to need him, because I have to tell you something. Brett has cancer.'

"Actually, she handled it better than I thought she would. She seemed so stunned that this could happen to their family again that we just cried together. I said, 'We'll get through this. God's not going to leave us now. He never has.'

"She said, 'I know, Eveline. I know.'

Then she asked to talk to Brett, and he managed a few whispers of encouragement."

We knew it wouldn't be long before the word got around. Perhaps it was naive to think we could somehow manage the release of the information, but we tried.

We were in for the experience of a lifetime.

THE CRUCIBLE OF PAIN

It's impossible to overstate the torture of recuperating from that tonsillectomy. I counted the minutes until my next dose of painkiller, though it barely seemed to dent the agony. There was no relief, no letup. I couldn't change positions or turn my head a certain way or try to sleep it off. The best I could hope for was a few minutes of dozing, but I always jerked awake, worried that my throat might have gone dry. Dryness was the worst.

I pleaded for heavier painkillers, morphine, anything. Eveline felt so sorry for me. She asked Bob if there wasn't something that would relieve the excruciating pain.

He said, "Brett, just make it to that ninth day. It will be like a miraculous healing. There's nothing we can do for you between now and the ninth day. You just have to endure it."

On top of the misery was the exhaustion of sleeplessness. It was nearly impossible to eat, and I was quickly losing weight. The pain even overwhelmed the news that I had cancer. But it couldn't subdue it enough. In my frustration, desperately at the end of myself, I finally vented to God.

Lord, I cried, *I'm not even thirty-nine yet. I've tried to live my life the way you wanted me to. I don't understand it. I don't smoke. What is going on? And what about Eveline and the kids? What's gonna happen to them?*

Suddenly I felt a subtle nudging in my spirit. It was as if God was impressing upon me, *You couldn't even start on your high school baseball team, and I put you in the big leagues for fifteen years. Trust me. And your wife and kids? You couldn't possibly love them nearly as much as I do.*

Lord, I continued, *what's my purpose? At least I have to have a purpose. Jesus had a purpose. Show me what mine is.*

While I was going through all that self-pitying and worrying about the future, Eveline was informing more of our loved ones. She remembers: "In the back of my mind I knew that Tim Brown, our reporter friend, was going to check back in sometime. With all the family and friends and all the medical personnel who knew about Brett's condition, the news was bound to leak out. I didn't want people to just hear it. We needed a statement that came directly from us.

"It just happened that in between phone calls, Tim Brown called. He said, 'How's our patient today?'

" 'He's doing okay,' I said. 'Tim, can you hold on a second?'

"I put him on hold and turned to Brett. 'It's Tim Brown. We've got to figure out how to release this to the press. I trust him and you trust him, so is it okay if I tell Tim?'

" 'Tell him,' Brett rasped, 'but tell him he can't tell anybody. He's got to hold it. He cannot release it to the paper until after we've told the team.'

"So I told Tim I was going to tell him something, but I had to have his promise he would not tell anybody or release it to the paper.

" 'What's going on?'

" 'Just promise me.'

" 'I promise.'

" 'When I told you Friday that there weren't any complications we knew about, that was the truth,' I said. 'But now we know that a tumor they found is cancerous.'

"Tim was blown away like a friend, not a reporter. He respected our wishes and we assured him he would have full access to Brett if he would cooperate with us. Then Brett and I worked on a statement and called the Dodgers so it could be released to the press and to the public."

Though I was in serious pain, I wanted our statement to be crystal clear. Eveline wrote it out as we worked on it. The final product read:

> My goal was always to play major-league baseball. I've been fortunate to accomplish that goal for sixteen years.
>
> Baseball is the foundation of my life and always will be. But even more than baseball, my faith in Christ is my strength and at the core of my being. We don't know why things like this happen, but we know that God's will is perfect.
>
> We have many friends in and out of baseball and this will come as a major shock. It is impossible to speak to all of them personally. My wife and I would ask for your prayers for us and our children at this difficult time. We're not sure where this road will lead us, but we will try our best to keep you informed.

The Dodgers were in Cincinnati. Eveline didn't want to risk faxing our statement to Derrick Hall, so she read it to him over the phone. Derrick called Tommy Lasorda, who called the coaches together. Then he closed the clubhouse and Tommy and Fred Claire told the players. Our first baseman, Eric Karros, outfielder Todd Hollandsworth, and several others cried when they heard the news.

Todd, whom I had gotten to know well when I came back to

the Dodgers from the Mets in 1995, is as close to me as a brother, though he's sixteen years younger. He played his first full year with the Dodgers in 1996 and was named Rookie of the Year in the National League. "I was devastated at the news of Brett's cancer," he says. "I didn't even want to play that day. When I stopped crying I was angry and wondered how God could let something like that happen to one of the strongest God-fearing men I knew. Later, I realized it wasn't God's doing. And he turned the turmoil into a great witness for himself." (Todd would hit two homers in that game, and yet he told me he still felt empty afterward.)

Later I got a letter from Todd that read:

> It is difficult for me to write this. Brett, you're one of my closest and dearest friends. You're an inspiration to me in ways you may not ever know. Your love, instruction, and advice have helped bring me to where I am now. This world is a scary place to me without you in it.
>
> This will pass in the twinkling of an eye, and I know that when it's all over your testimony will be so much greater and our Lord will be glorified. Be strong in the name of the Lord. My prayers will be with you and your family always.

The clubhouse meeting where my teammates were told I had cancer ended with prayer. Tommy Lasorda was quoted in the next day's paper, "It's hard when you love somebody so much, not only as a ballplayer but as a person. He's a member of the family. We can only hope he gets over this thing and lives a healthy life."

Roger Cedeno, the young outfielder I had encouraged to be so outstanding as my replacement that he would take over my job, told reporters, "That's why I cried so much when I found out about his cancer. Last night I couldn't even go to bed because I feel so bad. I hurt inside. I don't think I fell asleep until four in the morning. That guy, man, he was incredible. He was there for me. Now I want to make him proud."

Relief pitcher Todd Worrell, also a Christian, urged everybody to write personal messages to me. Milt Thompson wrote my number on his baseball spikes. He said, "We all plan to remember Brett in our special way. Believe me, he will never be forgotten."

Eveline remembers: "My best friend, Indy, came hobbling over one day with her foot in a cast. She had just had surgery. She's a speech therapist and knew that the most important thing at that time was to get Brett to swallow. Indy had her husband, Steve, carry over a picnic basket of foods that might help. We tried to get Brett to eat a little. Steve sat on one side of the bed, I sat on the other, and Indy sat there with her leg propped up on a pillow.

"Poor Brett was in such pain he could hardly move. Indy said to Steve, 'I guess this is the only time you'll let me be in bed with your best friend.'

"Steve and Indy and I cracked up, and I'm sure Brett would have thought that was funny, too, if he hadn't been in such misery. We were laughing so hard we made the bed bounce, while Brett was nearly crying from trying to swallow Indy's concoction."

One of the most moving things that happened to me that week was a gesture on the part of ten-year-old Cullen Robinson, Lowery and Vicki's son. When he was three years old, Cullen cut three fingers off in an electrical fan. When he had them sewn back on, I was playing my first game for the Giants, and I brought him the game ball. I can hardly believe he still remembers that, but when he found out I had cancer he told Lowery he was going to give me a game ball from one of his Little League games.

The problem was, he had already earned a game ball and each player was allowed only one game ball per season. He told his dad he was going to do something special so he could get another game ball somehow. His next game he struck out nineteen batters and hit a home run. That Little League game ball Cullen gave me means as much to me as any other memento in my trophy case.

While I was enduring my painful misery and trying to discover the purpose of all this, the doctors determined there was no link between my cancer and my limited use of smokeless tobacco fifteen years before. Still, because of my cancer, other players vowed to quit chewing and dipping. I decided that alone might be God's reason for letting me go through this. If those guys can quit that stuff the way I did, they'll keep a lot of youngsters from following their bad habits.

I quit when I was teaching a baseball clinic in Georgia in the early 1980s. A little boy was putting some dip in his mouth and told me he did it because, "You do it, and you're my hero."

"I'll make a deal with you," I said. "If you'll stop, I'll stop. You'll know I quit because when I come to bat, I'll be blowing bubbles."

I was grateful for the brief glimpses I was beginning to see of how God could use my illness to help others.

Another unforgettable day was when Eric Karros called to talk to me. He told Eveline he just wanted to say a few things to me. Later he told people he thought he was going to say something profound, but when he got on the phone he couldn't talk through his tears. I tried to encourage him, telling him that there was a reason for everything, but he said he sure couldn't see a reason for this.

There were so many dear friends that Eveline and I wanted to tell personally, but we just couldn't. We hated to have them hear the news secondhand, but there was no way around it. We have four phone lines coming into our house, and as the news started spreading, those lines rang and rang all day. Then the letters began pouring in. First it was hundreds, then thousands, then tens of thousands. Before the avalanche began to ebb, more than 180,000 letters had poured in. It was overwhelming. We couldn't answer them all, of course, but Eveline tried to thank all those who also sent a gift. (A small sampling of those letters can be found in Appendix I.)

*   *   *

On the ninth day of my recuperation from the tonsillectomy, I found that Dr. Bob was right. Suddenly, the pain slackened. It had been the longest nine days of my life.

During this time, Vince Nauss, head of Baseball Chapel, sent me a verse from Jeremiah. It says, "For I know the plans I have for you . . . plans to prosper you and not to harm you, plans to give you hope and a future" (Jer. 29:11 NIV). What an awesome verse! I kept it in my den and just kept reading it. Often I would simply pray, *I know that you know the plans you have for me, Lord.*

After a few days, when I saw the impact my problems were having on other people, I began to see that God could use this for his glory. That was all I wanted to know. I was willing to go through it and knew he had promised to stand by me through everything, but I just wanted a handle on what it was all about.

I told the Lord, *If I accept the good you give me, I can also accept the bad.*

I thanked him for the legacy of my father, and one of my dad's great statements came to mind: "The character of a man doesn't show when things are going good. It shows when things are going bad, in how you handle adversity."

Finally, I came to a point of peace. I prayed , *All right, Lord, just give me the strength to get through it, whatever it is, whether by death or in life.* Paul had written that, "For to me, to live is Christ and to die is gain" (Phil. 1:21 NIV). Now I understood what that meant.

From that point on, I felt there was a purpose for all this and that it was bigger than I was. Other people had had cancer, so why such an outpouring of love and affection for me? I wanted to follow God's lead and be sure he was glorified in all this, not me.

Eveline recalls: "One of our young friends, Mark Jones, called and asked if he could bring his pastor over to talk to Brett. He felt God had prompted him to do that. I had been turning down a lot of requests for people to see Brett. But for some reason, I spontaneously said yes. I don't know why.

"When I broke the news to Brett that a stranger was coming over, he looked at me as if I had betrayed him. I told him that Mark said God had prompted him, so Brett agreed. As soon as that pastor was in our home, I felt a real peace. I left Mark and him alone with Brett and they talked for an hour. When they left, Brett's entire personality and attitude had changed."

Somehow, what Mark's pastor said to me made sense. He told me he had been praying and that God had impressed upon him that I was going to be okay and that God was going to take this and use it in much more of a powerful way than I could ever conceive. That was a real turning point for me.

Next on the agenda was that Dr. Bob wanted me to go to Emory University Hospital where I would consult with Dr. William Grist. I had to have an MRI and schedule a neck dissection. He would go back into my throat and remove fifty lymph nodes, because they feared the cancer had spread.

Eveline says: "The day we took Brett over there, he was so sick he could barely breathe. They had put him on a heavy painkiller because he hurt so bad. We put him in the front seat to help guard against motion sickness. Lowery drove, following Dr. Bob, while Vicki and I sat in the back. By the time we got to Emory, bless his heart, Brett was ready to throw up in a trash can. I was glad Vicki was with me, because I needed someone to talk to. She said, 'This must be so hard on you.'

" 'It is,' I said. 'I feel as if at any moment I could lose it. To see him have to go through this is just too much. I look at people in the world, and I think there are a lot of really rotten people out there. But Brett's not that way. He's just so good. To see him suffer like this is killing me.'

" 'We'll get through it, Eveline,' Vicki said. 'It will be all right. Anytime you need to call me and just cry, do it.' "

I felt awful that day. When I went down for my MRI, Lowery and Vicki and Eveline and Dr. Bob were with me. Soon Steve Dils and his wife showed up. Steve had been a quarterback at Stanford and played in the NFL for ten years. Then one of my oldest spiritual advisers, Walt Wiley showed up. I had met him when he was doing a baseball chapel when I first broke into the big leagues in Atlanta in the early 1980s. He has been a mentor of mine ever since. His son Bart now works for us.

Dr. Grist studied the MRI and was a little surprised when he and Dr. Gerald Gussick came out to tell Eveline and me what he planned to do surgically. Here were all these friends and loved ones. He just plunged ahead. All I wanted to know was whether this surgery would be as bad as the tonsillectomy. He assured me it would not be.

I asked Dr. Grist, "Can I play baseball again?"

The doctor said, "Well, not this year."

"That's it. I'm done."

Eveline reacted quickly. "What do you mean?"

"I'm done. I'm finished. I'm going to retire. I'm not going to play again."

"Brett, listen," Eveline said. "Don't be Mr. Extremist, going from one thing to the other. Why don't you just wait and see? Let's get through this and see if you can play baseball. Then you can decide whether or not you want to. You don't need to make a decision today for something that may be six months away. Let's just take it one step at a time."

"No," I insisted, "I'm done."

Dr. Grist said, "Brett, your wife has some pretty good advice there. You will not play this year. It's impossible, but that doesn't mean you can't play next year. Once you're healed from this you will lead a normal, active life. You'll be fine."

He had hit my hot button. "Okay, then put a number on it."

"What do you mean?"

"Give me the odds against my playing this year."

"This year? No, you can't play this year."

I said, "Put a number on it. What are the odds?"

Dr. Grist sighed. "Okay, one in five thousand."

I looked at Eveline and forced a smile. "Those are pretty good odds. It was one in ten thousand that I'd ever get to the big leagues."

Eveline knew then that I had a challenge and that's what I needed. She knew I had to have somebody telling me I couldn't do something. Then I would go after it with everything I had in me.

A four-hour operation was scheduled for May 21, 1996, two weeks after I was informed I had cancer. It would be just seventeen days since the tonsillectomy.

The night before I went in for surgery, a group of my closest Christian brothers came over. Walt Wiley, his two sons Brett and Bart, Tim Cash, Lowery Robinson, Steve Cesari, Steve Dils, my brother Ben, and Greg McMichael and John Smoltz of the Braves showed up to pray for me. They applied oil to my forehead, laid their hands on me, and prayed over me. We told our wives we would be gone about forty-five minutes, but it was two-and-a-half hours. We were downstairs in my small, soundproof theater room, and it was boiling in there. We were all sweating. But it was an unbelievable time I will never forget. As those ten people who loved me laid their hands on me and prayed for me, it was as if God himself touched me. I wasn't miraculously healed or anything like that, but I had such a sense of peace and comfort and support. God had sent these men to minister to me. That two-and-a-half-hour prayer service, when we all sweat through our clothes, remains one of the highlights of my life.

Eveline and I couldn't believe the number of people who showed up at the hospital to see me through the cancer surgery. By the time I was ready to go into the operating room, it seemed every close friend and relative I had was there standing by me. Mickey Mellman of the Dodgers was there. My brother and sister were there. And all our dear friends from Atlanta.

I was put in a big beautiful suite of rooms that had been left to the hospital by wealthy Coca-Cola heirs. That made it easier for my family to be hospitable to everybody who came to see me.

As I was wheeled out to the operating room, with all their anxious eyes on me, I felt—even in my anesthetized state—that when it came to friends and loved ones, I couldn't be a wealthier man. Somehow I knew God would use that wealth of love to get me through all of this.

From my childhood I had been surrounded by love and support and discipline that had made me the man I was, going into surgery . . .

SHOW YOUR BUTLER CLASS

I knew better. I had been told and told never to play with matches.

It was Christmas morning, 1967. I was ten years old. My brother Ben was eight, my sister Beverly, five. Like most other kids, we were up long before our parents on that magical day. Mom had decorated the house for the holidays and there were candles all over the place. I got it in my head that the room would look a lot more Christmassy if those candles were lit. So I lit them.

I was right. The place looked great in the candlelight. Ben and Bev and I sat watching TV for a while, trying to make the time pass quickly before my parents got up and we could finally find out what was in all those beautifully wrapped presents under the tree.

If Mom and Dad got up while those candles were still burning, I knew I would be in deep trouble, so I enlisted Ben and Bev to help blow them all out.

A five-year-old girl is too young to know that she has to hold her hair back when leaning down to blow out a candle. The next thing I knew Bev's hair was on fire, she was screaming, and Mom came running, calling for my dad at the top of her lungs: "Jerry!"

I was close enough to clap out the fire with my hands and whisper desperately to my shrieking sister that she should tell Mom and Dad that the matting in her hair was candy.

My father immediately sized up the situation, and my heart sank when he said nothing. He merely went out to the garage, found a two-by-four, and set to work with his jigsaw. All too soon he returned with a custom-made paddle, holes in it to cut down on wind resistance, and plenty big enough to teach a hard lesson to two little boys.

Dad made Ben and me grab our ankles and lit into us good. Of course we screamed and cried and promised we'd never do such a foolish thing again, but Dad assured us we had not seen the end of that paddle.

"I'm sorry, boys," he said, "but every time I think of what could have happened to your sister's face, I'm going to spank you."

He kept to his word, as he always did. Several times that day he came to our bedroom, where we lay on our stomachs to keep from sitting on the welts, and he smacked us again. Once, during the afternoon, with friends over playing cards, Dad said, "You'll have to excuse me while I go beat my boys."

That incident has become a legend in our family. Some might call it child abuse today, but if ever a kid needed a whipping, I did for pulling that stunt. Poor Ben got punished just for not talking me out of it. I'll tell you this, it was effective. I don't believe I picked up another match until I was twenty-one years old.

My dad was a godly man. He was strict and a disciplinarian, and while I had a healthy fear of him, I also idolized him and considered him perfect. He's been gone since 1984, yet hardly a day goes by that I don't think of some bit of advice or counsel he gave me.

Not long ago I was driving back into Los Angeles on the 105

and noticed several lone drivers buzzing down the carpool lane, the one reserved for cars with multiple passengers. I knew I could get away with the same thing. In fact, had I been pulled over, an L.A. cop would probably recognize me and give me a break. But I couldn't do it. I wasn't raised that way. My mom and dad always said, "Show your Butler class, not your Butler _____."

They always spelled out that last word. I heard my dad actually cuss only twice in my life. Once, when I was twenty-one and home for the Christmas holidays, I came in after having had too much to drink. My grandmother was visiting, and my dad said, "I can't believe you're drunk in front of her."

"I'm not drunk, I'm fine."

"You're not fine," he said, "and I can't believe you would do this."

I said, "Ah, blow it off," and walked into my room. He followed me and closed the door.

"You know what?" he said. "If your grandmother wasn't here, I'd kick your a—."

Proving his point for him about my drinking, I threw my coat on the bed and said, "If you think you're so bad, let's get after it."

I still don't know how I could have said such a thing to the person I loved and admired more than anyone in the world, but I said it and it crushed him. He just looked at me with utter sadness in his eyes and said quietly, "I never thought the day would come where a son of mine would show me that kind of disrespect."

When he turned and walked away, it was the worst punishment I could have ever received. It was much worse than the paddling I'd gotten that Christmas more than a decade before. Devastated, I soon found him in his favorite easy chair, in front of the TV. I sat at his feet, sobbing. "I'm sorry, Dad. I love you. I'll never do that again."

For several days during that vacation, even after he had forgiven me, I cried and asked his forgiveness when I thought of how

I had spoken to him. Years later I brought it up to him, and, characteristically, he said, "Ah, I don't remember that."

The only other time I heard my dad cuss was a year after the first incident, when I called him after college graduation and said, "Dad, I've got good news and bad news. The bad news is I can't come home this summer. The good news is I've been drafted by the Atlanta Braves."

"No s——," my dad said. I was shocked. It had just slipped out. I said, "Dad!"

"I'm sorry, son," he said. "You just surprised me there."

He had surprised me too.

I still feel young, but I can't deny I was raised the old-fashioned way in an era that seems to have vanished. My mother was a stay-at-home mom until I was in high school, and even then she worked at the school I attended. We were a churchgoing family, and it seems every sage piece of advice I got from either Mom or Dad had some sort of a biblical root to it. My parents' version of the Golden Rule was, "Treat others as you wanted to be treated."

We were taught to honor our father and mother. A lot of my friends referred to their parents as their "old man" or "old lady." I never did. I wanted them to be proud of me always. My dad always said he wanted to be proud of me. I was proud of them. My mother died two years ago, but in my mind both my parents are still on a pedestal. My dad was a traveling salesman, gone from Monday morning until Friday night, and my mother's life was at home with us kids. My father was such a presence, however, I hardly remember him not being there for us. He was an ex-Marine, and my brother and I were taught that we should never start a fight or hurt anybody. But we were to defend ourselves. We fought each other, and I got in trouble once for knocking Ben out. Once, when I felt I had no choice but to punch a kid in the nose, I took him home and apologized to his parents.

My desire is to be liked by everybody I meet. My agent's wife, who is an attorney, has told me I'm one of the most insecure people she's ever met. "How so?" I asked her.

She said, "If you were in a room with a hundred people, ninety-nine of whom loved you and one who didn't, you'd spend all your time chasing that one person all over the room until you won him over."

I couldn't argue with that.

It stems from having always been the smallest kid around, the last chosen for sports teams, and always having something to prove. For as long as I can remember, I have used negative input for positive motivation. There may have been times, way back when, when I wished I was bigger and stronger, but I don't remember that. I was always determined, always optimistic, always convinced that the glass was half full, not half empty. I knew I had the confidence and love and support of my parents, and somehow that made me eager to prove to everyone that I could do anything the bigger kids could do. At the risk of sounding immodest, I am convinced that attitude played a big part in getting me all the way to the major leagues and keeping me there for seventeen seasons. A person's mental attitude can be a powerful thing.

My mother had every bit as much influence on me as my father did. To me, the two of them could do no wrong. They were the epitome of what parents should be. What they said went. Most important was the fact that they lived what they believed. My mother instilled in me that God loves children. That was a big thing in our household. Somehow I knew God was going to take care of me and that he was my friend. Mom lived this out in the way she loved us.

Every single day during my elementary school years my mother waited for me at the corner, carried my books, and raced me home. I never beat her. Not once. A grown woman, carrying schoolbooks, and she beat me every time! In my professional career I became a base stealer, and I trace that skill all the way back to trying vainly to catch my mother, running home from school.

Mom was totally family oriented, and that has rubbed off on me. I've told people, and I mean it, that even if I managed to hit .400 this year and wound up named Most Valuable Player in the National League, it's still my last year. My biggest investment is in my kids' lives, the same as it was for my mother.

Mom came by that naturally. Her own mother was an orphan who married young to get out of the orphanage. She had six kids before she found the true love of her life. She took her three oldest and went to California, leaving the younger three back east. My mother, one of those left behind, hitchhiked across the country at twelve years of age to find her mother. The family unit, taking care of each other, the family being the most important thing—that was what my mother lived for.

My mother was very strict and disciplined about church attendance and mealtime prayers. She would sit down and walk us through everything. She told us Bible stories. She asked us, "What would Jesus do? If Jesus were standing here, what would he do?" We were instructed to live in such a way that we did the right thing. No matter what our friends did, no matter what the peer pressure, we were to make sure we would do what Jesus would do. I have never forgotten that. I haven't always done it, but that lesson ringing in my ears has eventually brought me back to where I needed to be. My desire was never to let my parents down, and I don't want to let my kids down either.

I was born at Good Samaritan Hospital in downtown Los Angeles in 1957, and for the first couple of years of my life, we lived off Alvarado Street, not far from where Dodger Stadium was built at Chavez Ravine five years later. It's funny how life has a way of coming back around. From there we moved to Fremont, California, across the Bay from San Francisco. My father was a salesman for a company called Anchor Coupling, which manufactured hydraulic hoses.

One of the ways my father lived out his philosophy of life was by taking in the troubled children of his relatives. One of my mother's brothers, my Uncle Bob, stayed with us when he was a teenager. He was a hell-raiser, but under my father's disciplined tutelage he became a respectable, mature young adult. To this day, we're very close.

One of my father's cousins, who had two daughters, died in my father's arms. The last thing he said was, "Jerry, take care of my girls." My dad was a man of his word. One of those girls went off and got married. The other got into all sorts of trouble, was sent to juvenile hall, got straight Fs in high school, and eventually came to live with us for a year. During that time her life was turned around. Her grades improved. I remember she once brought a guy home to meet my dad, because Dad said he had to approve her dates. Dad told this guy he could only go out with her if he cut his hair. She took him into the bathroom and gave him a haircut. I don't know what ever happened to that relationship, but to this day she says the most precious time of her life was the year she spent with us.

That's how my father was. Anyone who needed something got it, if Dad had it. And he didn't have much. He lived paycheck to paycheck. Even when Eveline and I got married, Dad gave us the five hundred dollars he had in his savings account. That's the kind of man he was—the kind I want to be. Though I believe that God's timing is always perfect, the biggest regret of my life is that my father died when my oldest daughter was sixteen months old. He never got to know his grandchildren, and he would have blessed them. They always ask about him. If only they could have known him.

My mother was not the only person I couldn't beat in a race when I was a kid. I met my best friend for life, Dave Hinman, before we started kindergarten, when his family moved into the house right around the corner from us. His dad was a teacher, and twice during my childhood, they moved away, first to Micronesia

and then to American Samoa. Other than that, we were insepara-
ble. I feel fortunate to be able to say I have several dear friends,
but none go back as far with me as Dave. We never had to tell each
other the highlights of our lives. We lived them together. When we
had milk and cookies at rest time during kindergarten, our mats
were right next to each other. Even though Dave attended the
school where his father taught when he was in first, second, and
third grades, we spent every other spare minute together.

Apparently I was a hyper kid. I don't remember this, but my
mother used to tell me that I was so full of energy, my early grade
teachers used my belt to anchor me to my desk. One told my
mother that it didn't matter if I was just an average student. "He'll
get by on personality alone," she said.

I don't remember Dave being that hyper, but otherwise we
were like twins. To this day we're virtually the same size. I may not
see him for months, but when we hear each other's voice on the
phone, we just pick up where we left off.

Dave and I made a pact when we were six years old that we
would both become big-league baseball players. I don't know
when or where I saw my first baseball game, but as soon as I signed
up for peewee baseball at age six and got my little uniform, I was
locked in. There was no turning back. I not only wanted to be a
big leaguer, I knew without a shadow of a doubt that I would be.
Nothing would get in my way. Dave and I would gather the neigh-
borhood kids during the summer and play literally from dawn
until lunchtime, and then from after lunch until it got so dark our
parents called us home. If allowed, we would have played in the
black of night, never going home voluntarily.

I've heard others say, and I agree, that the problem with baseball today is that kids don't play anymore unless they have a uniform on. Playing in uniform with our teams every few days was just
icing on the cake. At all other times, we played among ourselves,
all day long. We had to get up early in the summertime, or we'd be

left without a field to play on. Today, though, many fields through-out America are empty.

In that kind of sandlot baseball, you could come to the plate as many times in one day as you did in a whole Little League season. You could play every position, field as many grounders and fly balls, and run as many bases as you would in a year of organized baseball. We weren't doing it with the purpose of logging all those speeds and angles into our brains or building muscle memory for various kinds of plays and throws, but who knows what all that might have contributed to my future as a ballplayer? We just played because we loved the game.

Because I was so small, if I hadn't organized the game or if I was new to the group that was playing, I was usually one of the last chosen—just like Dave. We were the little guys. The only thing was, once the game started, people took notice. We could play.

We played on teams together all the way up through Little League, traveling with all-star teams, playing in tournaments, you name it. I thought catching was one avenue to the big leagues, so I was probably the only left-handed catcher most people had ever seen. I've played baseball every summer since I was six years old.

Dave would get into other things as he got older. He's now a custom home builder. But I know he enjoys my baseball career as if he's right there with me. Because, in his heart, he is.

THE
ANNOUNCEMENT

All I knew was Fremont, California. I never thought of living anywhere else. To me it seemed I had the perfect life. My best friend, Dave, and I were blood brothers and spent as much time at each other's house as we did at our own. Dave remembers that almost every time he came to my house for lunch, we had melted cheese sandwiches. We still laugh about the time my mother took out her dental plate and showed him her gums.

Dave and I did everything together. When one of us would decide that life was simply unbearable at home, we'd run away. Of course we ran to the other's house. I remember one time being pretty serious about it and getting about five blocks from home before turning around and seeing my mother standing there waiting for me. I ran back crying.

I was thrilled to be a Brave in the peewee baseball league and quickly became obsessive about my uniform. Everything had to be just right—shoes shined, laces even, socks and stirrups just so, pant stripe straight, shirt carefully tucked in, cap bill curved just the way I liked it. I wanted to look like a big leaguer from day one.

When we got to go to an Oakland Athletics game, we sat in the left field stands with Reggie's Regimen, where we cheered our heads off for Reggie Jackson. Sometimes we watched the San Francisco Giants and made sure everybody around us knew that Jim Davenport went to our dentist. Knowing he got his teeth worked on in the same chair I did almost made me a big leaguer.

Dave's and my parents bowled together, so we kids spent a lot of time at the bowling alleys. (My mother became quite good, ranking fourth in the state by the time I was in high school.) I've told Eveline that one thing I'm going to do when I get out of baseball is to get on a bowling team.

When Dave was seven years old, he got a set of golf clubs. Of course they were for a right-hander. I couldn't let him get ahead of me in any sport, so I learned to play golf right-handed and still do. It's the only sport I play right-handed. To this day Dave and I are still very competitive when we get a chance to play golf with each other.

Dave and I ate, drank, and slept baseball. On Friday nights one of us usually slept over at the other's house, and in the morning we got up and watched the baseball Game of the Week and kept score. We knew more baseball statistics before we were ten years old than most kids know in high school today. That was our life. We lived close to Irvington High School, so we'd hop the fence and play on their field. We were always playing something. Mostly baseball. We got into very little trouble because we were so busy.

One day when we were six, Dave and I climbed the fence to watch a high school game. I was quite enamored of the high school players and their beautiful uniforms. While watching the game, I didn't realize how close I had wandered to a player taking his practice swings. His follow-through caught me just above the eye and opened a gash in my forehead. He felt so bad he scooped me up and carried me to my house.

"I'm sorry, Mrs. Butler," he said. "I didn't see him behind me."

My mother gathered me in her arms to assess the damage, and all I could say was, "Look, Mom, I got carried home by a baseball player."

My parents kept a picture of me, taken when I was eight, in my Braves uniform. A few years ago a trading card company used it as one of my cards. Whenever I see it I'm reminded of the time my dad saw me shy away from a ball during a game. That afternoon he stood me in front of the garage door and began firing balls at me, making me stand there and catch them.

He drew closer and closer and threw harder and harder, but somehow, rather than feeling scared or intimidated, I loved the challenge. It made me mentally tough. The balls hit me a few times and they stung, but just like Dad said, "It never hurts for long."

I learned quickly that I could catch those balls if I didn't back away. Soon I was not afraid of the ball in the least.

I hated it when Dave moved away again for a year and a half when we were in fifth grade. But we had a great family. My brother and sister and I were close. The whole family went to church every Sunday, and Sunday afternoons were just for the family. We weren't allowed to go anywhere, and we didn't want to. We stayed at home and played all kinds of games—and we still do when we get together, though we miss our parents so much.

I got a paper route when I was in sixth grade and what I remember most about it was that my mom would get up before dawn and help me roll and band those papers before I went out to deliver them. She didn't have to do that. She was just that kind of mom.

My favorite memories of childhood are of those weekday mornings at 5:30 when it was just Mom and me. She would make me a little breakfast, then we would roll my papers and I would go throw my route. On the way back every day I would stop at Winchell's Donut Shop and get a hot chocolate and a cream-filled long john. Either of those tastes today brings back melancholy memories of Mom and my paper route.

When Dave moved back to Fremont, he and I were old enough to get into a little more mischief. Once he and Ben and I went to the Alex Shopping Center on Carol Avenue in Fremont and shoplifted some golf balls from the sporting goods store. Dave and I each put a three-ball sleeve down our pants. Ben wouldn't do it.

Not much later we were at the high school across the street from my house, hitting those golf balls all over the place. Pretty soon my mother called us over. "Brett," she said, "the manager of the sports store at the Alex Shopping Center called. He said he knows you guys stole those golf balls and unless you come back and pay for them, you're going to jail."

We were so scared we burst into tears and bawled our eyes out.

Mom drove us back there. Dave and I hurried to the manager. "Mister," I said, "we're sorry. We didn't mean anything by it. Here's the money."

He seemed startled by it all, and I didn't learn until about five years ago that my mother had made that story up. Ben had told her we stole the golf balls, but she knew if she said that, we'd take it out on him. I'll never forget calling Dave to tell him, "Remember way back when at the Alex Shopping Center? It was Ben who ratted on us!"

My poor sister had to go to every one of Ben's or my games, and all we had to do was go to Beverly's annual dance recital. It didn't seem fair and it probably wasn't, though she says now that she's glad for all the baseball she learned back then. It makes me feel good to know she still enjoys watching me play.

Ben was a couple of years behind us, of course, but Dave and I were lucky enough to play on some really good teams and share a lot of all-star experiences together. In the summer of 1969, when I was twelve, I played on a great team called the Teamsters 768. One of our pitchers was six feet tall and I had to catch him, even though I was left-handed, because I was the only one who could. When he wasn't pitching, someone else caught and I played in the outfield.

Our coach was a man named Marty Enriquez. On my first major-league trip to San Francisco seventeen years ago, I looked him up. He and his wife recognized me immediately, even though they hadn't seen me for ten years. We had a great reunion.

My Little League hat was a big deal. I wore it almost all day, every day, that summer back in 1969. It fit as if I had been born wearing it, and it carried the pins signifying the all-star teams I had played on.

Not long before the all-star game that season, my cousin Mark, who is just a few months older than me, was visiting. We were racing our bikes and somehow I flipped over my handlebars and landed on my chin. I whipped my cap off to catch the gushing blood, then quickly realized I cared more about that hat than my chin. The bone was exposed and my mother had to drive me to the emergency room for stitches, but the most important thing to me was that I had not ruined my hat. Unfortunately, I missed the all-star game.

That fall, Dave and I entered seventh grade together. We were still determined to become big leaguers and we often talked about how we would be best friends forever. "I hope you don't have to move again," I said.

"Me too," he said.

"We're never going to move," I said. "You and I will always be together."

I got to thinking about how sure I was of that and decided I'd better check with my dad. I had been so young when we moved from Los Angeles to Fremont that I remembered nothing about it. Fremont was the only hometown I had ever known.

There had been times, I knew, when my father had considered

getting off the road as a traveling salesman and moving up in the company. But he preferred the road.

I asked him, "Dad, are we ever going to move?"

"No," he said. "It doesn't look like it. Things are going fine."

About a month later I was sitting in the house late one Friday afternoon when my dad came in from work. He came through the door without greeting anyone and walked straight to the bedroom. My mother looked alarmed and followed him. I followed her and when my mother opened the door I peeked in and saw my father on his knees. Mom closed the door. By now Ben and Beverly were wondering what was up too.

In a little while, when Mom and Dad emerged from the bedroom, Dad sat us down. "I've prayed about this," he said. "I feel God wants us to do this. We're moving to Libertyville, Illinois."

"Dad!" I said. "You told me we'd never move!"

"I know," he said. "But this is good. It will put me in the central office and give me an opportunity to be home more. There's nothing I want to do more than be home with you."

As shocking as that was, and as long as it took me to get used to the idea of leaving the only home I had ever known, privately I agreed it sounded great. Dad said he would be gone only about two days a week and would be able to get more involved in Little League and all our other activities.

Dad assured me I would not have to lose track of Dave. All four of my grandparents lived in California, so that's where our vacations would be spent. Nearly every summer after that I spent a few weeks with Dave.

There were down sides to moving to Illinois, of course. I hate cold and I hate snow, and we moved in the middle of winter. Libertyville is a northern suburb of Chicago, and 1970 proved to be a very snowy winter. I remember snowdrifts so deep that we had to shovel out the driveway every day and people tied flags on their car antennas so they could be seen coming around the twelve-foot piles of snow at the corners.

It hadn't been so bad being the smallest kid for my age in California, because most of the time Dave was with me and he was pretty small too. But now I was in a big suburb of a big city, and junior high schoolers always need someone to pick on. I was the perfect foil. I was made fun of for everything from my size to the fact that I wore white socks like a Californian instead of dark socks like a Midwesterner. I was called Surfer Boy and the Shoe Shine Kid because of my socks.

We lived close to Highland Junior High School, which was good for me. I had permission to leave the school grounds at lunchtime and go home. The other kids had to stay on school property. As soon as the bell rang, I flew out the door and outran all the guys who wanted to give me a wedgie. That procedure goes by different terms in different places, but it's basically the same everywhere: the goal was to reach down the back of my pants and yank my underwear up as far as possible. Every day for the rest of seventh and all of eighth grade, I was chased to the edge of the school property—during recess, lunchtime, and after school. But I was given a snuggie, or a Melvin, or a wedgie (whatever you want to call it) only one time. That was enough. They would not catch me again. I trace a lot of my adult speed to all those junior high escapes.

I knew I would quit getting hassled so much and start to develop a few friends once I was able to prove myself in sports. One of the first things I did was to lie to the basketball coach and tell him I had been captain of my team back in California. That got his attention and got me a spot on the team until I was able to learn enough to earn it. Of course, I was small for a guard and always got the smallest uniform, usually number two. That was appropriate, because there was always somebody telling me I was too small, too weak, too this, or too that. I became friends with the other guard, Aidis Kozica, but the one I beat out approached me at my locker one day. He tapped me on the shoulder and when I turned around he punched me in the stomach as hard as he could. I doubled over, groaning, as he hurried away. I couldn't wait to get to practice that day. I was going to kill him. I didn't want to fight, but he had started it, and I was going to finish it. Somehow, the coach got wind of it and announced before practice that anyone caught fighting would be kicked off the team. No revenge was worth that, I decided.

When the snow began to melt, I couldn't wait for baseball season. In the meantime I got another paper route. This one required one of those huge baskets on the front of my bike. A bully named Jim pushed my bike over and scattered my papers every day when I got to his house. It made me so mad I cried every time and wanted revenge, but I was too small and he was too big. I wasn't about to tell on him, and I couldn't skip his house. Five years later, when we were both seniors at Libertyville High School, I happened to walk by when Jim appeared to be restraining a girl against the lockers. I had been brought up to respect women. Here was my chance. I tapped him on the shoulder and said, "Jim?"

When he turned around, I punched him in the mouth as hard as I could hit him. As he was crumbling to the floor, I said, "That's for seventh grade. Anyway, you don't treat women like that."

I believed baseball would be my ticket to acceptance. With few friends, my brother and I spent a lot of time together. That was good for our relationship, and my mother appreciated it because of her bedrock emphasis on family.

I was getting tired of being the smallest and the weakest and always being picked on, but I decided not to let it make me angry. I didn't know if I would ever be a big person, but I was determined not to let that stand in the way of my dream. Being small and having to prove myself became the fiber of my being. I became focused and driven. I tried to excel at all sports and enjoyed showing people what I could do. But regardless of the season, regardless of the weather, regardless of the sport, my secret dream and desire was to become a big-league baseball player. I never doubted I would make it, and no setback ever made me wonder if I was deluding myself. This was not a pipe dream. This was a journey. There might be obstacles and bumps and even a few wrong turns along the way, but nothing would keep me from my goal.

For all the negatives involved in the move from California to Illinois, it was great that my dad was able to take me to the first baseball tryouts. I filled out a sheet that said I hit and threw left-handed, so they were surprised when I also said I was a catcher. I knew catching was one of the most difficult things to do and that very few guys could do it, so I thought it might be a way to set myself apart from the rest of the crowd. Wanting to test me, one of the tryout coaches said, "Why don't you go out and take a couple of fly balls."

I had to race and dive for the flies they hit me, but I caught them both. The coaches turned to my father. "He's a catcher all right," one of them said.

I made the Libertyville VFW team for thirteen, fourteen, and fifteen year olds. I would turn thirteen that June and be the youngest starter on our team. I played center field.

If you visit that field today, you'll see a picture of me in the concession stand and a tree planted there in memory of my mother.

That's where it all started, where I proved that if they'd just give me a chance, I'd show them. And I did. That's been the story of my life, and God has had his hand in it all the way.

FIVE

THE EIGHTY-NINE-POUND WEAKLING

When I entered Libertyville High School as a fourteen-year-old freshman in the fall of 1971, I was five feet tall and weighed eighty-nine pounds. Anybody predicting a future in sports for me would have guessed I would become a jockey. My biggest fear was that I would not grow enough by the time I got my driver's license to be able to see over the steering wheel. Somehow even that fear did not deter me from my big-league goal. I simply wondered how I would get back and forth to the airports and the stadiums. Would someone have to drive me? Would I have to use some sort of a booster seat?

As any other self-respecting jock would do, the first thing I did was to try out for football. Fortunately, the coach, Pat Summers, was a little guy like me. He didn't hold my size against me. The only place he could put me was in the backfield, so I played a lot of quarterback. My number? Two, of course. Too small, too weak. I had to roll out just to see past the big linemen, but I was scrappy enough to get the job done. My voice hadn't changed yet, so I heard a lot of mimicking of my falsetto, "Hut one! Hut two!"

THE EIGHTY-NINE-POUND WEAKLING

That winter I really wanted to play basketball, but I was also looking for a sport where I could earn a varsity letter as soon as possible. I wouldn't let my height get in my way when baseball season rolled around, but I had to be realistic about basketball. There were already several freshman a foot taller than I was.

My dad said, "Son, if you want to get a varsity letter, you ought to go out for wrestling."

Now there was a sport where underclassmen could wrestle on the varsity *because* of their size. The lower weight classes often had lots of freshmen and sophomores in them. Another freshman, Bill Whitmore, made the varsity in the lightest weight class, ninety-eight pounds. That encouraged me, because although I was on the junior varsity team, we were supposed to be able to challenge the varsity wrestler in our weight class every week. The winner would then wrestle in the varsity match. For some reason, however, the varsity coach would not allow me to challenge Bill that first year. I never understood why, and it made me mad.

When I was a sophomore I finally got to challenge him. The winner would wrestle in the 98-pound weight class, and the loser would move up to the 105-pound division. For nearly three years, Bill never beat me. Week after week we had our challenge match for the 98-pound starting spot (for which I was actually a little underweight), and I would win every time. By the time we were seniors we were challenging each other for the 119-pound class, with the loser moving up to the 126-pound class. Before one of those senior challenge matches, word came that Bill's father had been killed in a car wreck. I felt so bad I didn't have the heart to beat him. When he won, he got mad. He insisted on wrestling again, knowing that I had let him win.

As a sophomore and junior wrestler, I had been better than average. When I was a senior, I thought I would go all the way to the state meet. I got pinned in my first match but had a great season. I might have gone down state, but it all came crashing down with a shoulder separation. I had finished second in the conference meet, losing a disputed match to a kid I had beaten a week before, 15-3.

Ironically, wrestling became my best sport in high school. My highest highs and lowest lows were in that sport. I'll never forget standing on the second-place tier, crying my eyes out in rage and disappointment at not reaching my championship goal. But I knew things always happened for a reason.

I earned a varsity letter in wrestling the last three years, but I truly lived for baseball. As a freshman and sophomore I started and played the outfield for the frosh-soph teams, again under Pat Summers. I was better than average for my size, but I wasn't the star. Inside I kept alive my dream of being a major-league baseball player. I had learned not to talk about that too much. People would only laugh at me and tell me I was living in a dream world.

I soon gave up football during the fall season and took up cross country to get in shape for wrestling. Small as I was, I was growing. Often I starved myself or worked out extra hard and tried to sweat off a few pounds before my weigh-ins. Had I known more about health and nutrition and my own body, I would not have risked stunting my adult growth. Who knows how big I might have grown had I not unknowingly abused my body like that?

Being a small athlete in a large school with huge teammates and always having something to prove contributed to mental toughness. Basically I was a fun-loving kid, getting into mischief, cheating in Spanish, even streaking through the cafeteria with a couple of buddies one time.

It was around that time that God used Brice Elliott in my life. I had met him the year before playing football. By spring of our sophomore year in 1973, he and I had become good friends. During spring break his family was going to Colorado for a vacation. "I'm going to a Fellowship of Christian Athletes conference in Fort Collins," Brice said. "You want to come? There'll be lots of sports and messing around and races and stuff like that."

That sounded fantastic and I was thrilled when my parents said

I could go. Fort Collins was beautiful, and I enjoyed being on the campus of Colorado State University. The FCA conference was fun. They divided the guys into what they called huddle groups. Each huddle played sports against the others, ran relays, stayed together in the dorm, and had Bible studies and devotions together. I was amazed at how close we got to each other in just those few days. By the end of the week we would be crying as we said our farewells.

Every evening after dinner FCA held a huge meeting in an auditorium. We had music and a guest speaker. I don't even remember who he was, but each night he challenged us to examine our relationship to God.

I considered myself okay. I knew I had weak areas in my life, but I believed in God. I believed in Jesus. I had always thought that you try to do the best you can, you fail, you pick yourself up, and you start over. Like most people, I thought that if my good deeds outweighed my bad at the end of my life, I would make it to heaven. In my mind, that made me a Christian.

But one night the speaker really got to me. I don't know what was different this time, but I couldn't take my eyes off him. When he started quoting Bible verses to make his point, it was as if God was talking directly to me. He said a person could not expect to earn his way to heaven by doing good deeds. He said that there is no righteous person, not even one. All have sinned and come short of God's standard. All our righteousness is as filthy rags. I was beginning to feel guilty. Wasn't I a good guy? I had never hurt anyone. I could be selfish and short-tempered at times, and there were personal habits I needed to work on, but wasn't I basically an okay person? If I couldn't get to heaven by having my good days outnumber my bad, how was I supposed to get there? He quoted the famous verse, John 3:16, "For God so loved the world that He gave His only begotten Son, that whoever believes in Him should not perish but have everlasting life."

Then 1 John 1:9, "If we confess our sins, He is faithful and just to forgive us our sins and to cleanse us from all unrighteousness."

Then the speaker really hit close to home. He asked, "If you were to die right now, would you go to heaven?" Had he asked that before quoting all those other verses, I probably would have said yes. Now it seemed he was looking at and speaking directly to me. "Do you know beyond a shadow of a doubt that if you died tonight you would go to heaven?"

When he quoted Revelation 3:20, it really got to me. These were the words of Jesus. "Behold, I stand at the door and knock. If anyone hears My voice and opens the door, I will come in to him and dine with him, and he with Me."

The speaker said that door was the door of my heart. I wanted desperately to be certain that I was really a Christian and that I was assured of heaven. When the speaker asked guys to raise their hands if they wanted to receive Christ and make a commitment to him, I wanted to do that too, but not in front of all those guys. I couldn't wait for that meeting to be over so I could get back to the dorm and pray in private.

As soon as the meeting ended I ignored my new friends and raced outside, sprinting across the campus to my dorm room. All the way I pleaded with God not to let me get struck by lightning and killed before I had a chance to make sure I would go to heaven if I died. No one was around. I slipped into a closet and fell to my knees. *Lord,* I prayed, *I believe you are who you say you are, and I want to know beyond a shadow of a doubt that I'm yours and that I'll go to heaven when I die. I know I'm a sinner and that I fall short of your standard. I claim the promise that you're knocking at the door and if I open it you'll come in to me. I'm opening that door, Father. I want you in my life more than anything in the world.*

That was it. No bells, no thunder, just peace. I had acknowledged that God was who he said he was, that I was separated from him by my sin, and that I wanted to accept his forgiveness and to receive him into my heart.

From that moment to this, God has been sifting my life. I found that he would take from me and give me victory over anything I was willing to give up. My temper, my language, my dishonesty—he helped me with all those things. Have I lived a perfect life since then? Not even close. God had a lot of work to do on me, and he still does. Sometimes I've borrowed back areas I have given to him, and then the process starts all over again.

The toughest thing for me to give up, and one of the greatest strongholds of sin in my life, was my relationships with women. I knew I couldn't go on that way, especially calling myself a Christian, and I began praying that God would bring his choice of a permanent mate into my life.

For the rest of my high school years, I often felt like a hypocrite. I knew God was at work in my life because I could see the results. I also knew that I was holding out a few areas just for myself.

Having played on the Libertyville freshman and sophomore teams, I became a benchwarmer on the varsity as a junior. I may have had a few at bats and a few innings in the field that season, but mostly I kept score for Coach Ernie Ritta and spent a lot of time fraternizing with the cheerleaders.

During my senior year, 1974–75, I ran cross country in the fall, wrestled in the 119-pound level in the winter, and then almost immediately gained thirty pounds to play baseball again in the spring.

I had not been big enough or strong enough or impressive enough to have a legitimate complaint about riding the bench as a junior, but I was convinced if I got my chance as a senior, I could be a starter on the varsity. Coach Ritta did not agree.

Talk to anybody on the bench of any baseball team and you'll find a player who believes he should be in the starting lineup. Only the occasional role player realizes that he is there for utility purposes and accepts his place with grace. Managers and coaches don't want second stringers to be satisfied with their roles, as a rule. You want someone who's hungry, who believes in himself, and who is always itching to get in there and play.

I can't say I was angry that I hardly played at all on the varsity my senior year. Just a few months before I had been wrestling in the 119-pound weight class. Simply by ending my starvation diets and my killer workouts, I had put on the thirty pounds. But I was still seen as too small, too weak, too whatever.

Still, I felt I could play. I had a great arm, better than I have now. But the starting center fielder was the brother of our catcher, who was the best player. Our coach loved that catcher, though his brother did not deserve to start ahead of me. But what could I say?

Occasionally I found things to say. Once I told Coach Ritta, "Just let me play and I'll show you I deserve to start."

He would put me in the last few innings for defensive purposes. With my speed and my glove, he knew he could count on me out there. When I did get a few chances to hit, he usually called on me to bunt. It's what people expected from "the little guy." I was always the one whose mother had to take in my pants and make my uniform fit, no matter what sport I was in. Nobody who saw me play, even at the end of the season when I excelled, would have given you a nickel for my chances to become a major leaguer. All that just went into my storage tank, that reserve of will and determination I call on when I need motivation to prove myself yet again.

Through all of this, my father also believed I had a future in baseball. As was so often the case, he had the right thing to say. He used to tell me, "Son, if you don't believe in yourself, no one else will. Don't let anybody tell you that you can't do it. You go out there and do the very best you possibly can so you can look at yourself in the mirror and be satisfied, whether you make it or not, that you did everything you could."

I loved everything about baseball. I was the first one to practice and the last one to leave. I ran hard in every sprint. I followed through on every drill. I took all the hitting, fielding, throwing, and base-running practice I could get. But still I rode the bench.

The Libertyville Wildcats had a great baseball team that year. It would have been fun to have played on it all season. We were 15-2 going into the Illinois High School Association regional baseball tournament championship game against Zion-Benton High School. They had handed us our only two losses of the season. Coach Ritta started me in right field, telling local sportswriters that I was "a defensive replacement." We were facing an undefeated pitcher, and frankly I couldn't wait. You can always tell who the real "gamers" are on a ball team. They're the ones who don't cringe and grimace and find small injuries to keep them out of the lineup when they're facing the great pitchers in the league. Gamers are the ones who look forward to that kind of a challenge. I've always felt a hitter had nothing to lose in those situations. No one expects you to succeed anyway, so you may as well go up there and take your hacks.

We were leading Zion 3-0 in the top of the fifth when I drove a single (my second of the game) up the middle and scored a runner from second. Zion scored a couple of runs in the bottom of the sixth inning of the seven-inning game, but any hopes they had of overtaking us in the last inning ended with our rally in the top of the seventh. We had scored a run and had a runner on second with one out when I got my third hit of the game, a smash over the center fielder's head for a home run that rolled all the way to a backstop 460 feet from the plate.

Three days later, in a conference game against Dundee, I was again used as a "defensive replacement" because our left-handed ace pitcher was on the mound. I went 3-for-3 again, this time with a three-run homer and two singles, and we won 8-1.

Heading into the state sectional play-offs, we were one of only twenty-eight teams left in the hunt for the state championship. Suddenly, I was a starter. Coach Ritta mentioned me as one of his "three good outfielders." I was hitting .400, but I had been to the plate only twenty-five times the whole season. I had ten hits, two of them home runs. So much for my dreams of a college baseball scholarship. We lost in the sectionals, but I had played enough to earn my varsity baseball letter. Then came the athletic banquet and a watershed moment that helped prepare me to be mentally strong.

Our assistant coach, Jim Panther, who had played pro ball and is now the head coach at Libertyville, asked me during dinner what my college plans were. I told him I wanted to go to the best baseball school in the country, Arizona State University.

"You'll be a walk-on in a very tough program, Brett," he said. "I wish you all the best."

When it came time for each player to be recognized individually and receive his letter, I quickly found out that word had gotten back to Coach Ritta of my plans. He had been telling all the highlights of the team's stars and mentioning where several of them were going on baseball scholarships. Then he said, "and Brett Butler is going to Arizona State!"

As I walked up to get my varsity letter, he said, "Butler hardly played for me and he thinks he's going to play at Arizona State."

There were a few chuckles and my ears burned as I shook his hand and received my letter. I was the smallest guy on the team. I had batted fewer times than almost everyone there. No one saw me as a star. No one saw me as a scholarship player. No one expected me to even play in college. But I was going to be a big leaguer, and I knew it. I caught my father's eye, and he winked. It was our secret.

Dad told me he would pay for my first two years of college, but after that I was on my own. I knew I needed to go some place where I could show my stuff and get help from a good baseball program. Maybe it was crazy to go to a baseball power like ASU, but I believed if I got a chance, I could shine against the best competition in the country.

That summer I played American Legion ball in Libertyville.

When we played against Zion I renewed an acquaintance I had made with a good infielder, named Bobby Harju, from their high school team. We used to greet each other after games. I had done so well against them that he thought I was one of the Libertyville stars. I didn't know it then, but he would become one of those pivotal people in my life.

CHASING
THE DREAM

Like many other fathers, my dad always told me that as long as I lived under his roof and was under eighteen years old, I had to follow his rules. Those rules had not proved terribly confining. We had what I thought was a fun and close family. We played a lot, laughed a lot, and supported each other.

When my eighteenth birthday rolled around during that summer of 1975, I told my dad that what I really wanted was a big, all-night party with my buddies. To my surprise, he approved. His only rule was that no one could leave our house before morning.

We had a great time, and Dad's blessing made me feel like an adult. I knew that because he was financing my first two years of college, I would still be under his authority when I was home for visits, but he was good about loosening the reins and letting me learn some lessons the hard way.

My parents wanted me to attend Indiana State University, which was closer to home. My dad thought he might be able to wrangle me a combination wrestling and baseball scholarship. Maybe he could have, but my heart was set on Arizona State. Jim

Brock was the legendary coach there who had groomed many big-league players, probably more than any coach except Rod Dedeaux of Southern Cal. Dad reminded me that if I didn't work my way into a scholarship at Arizona State, I would be on my own financially during my last two years. I asked him if he still thought I had a chance of making the majors. He believed in me, that's all he would say. "Preparation meets opportunity, Brett," he said. "I've always told you that. If you're prepared, then you'll capitalize on that opportunity when it comes. You'll be able to do it if it's meant to be."

"Dad, I know you want me to go to Indiana State, but I want to go to ASU."

Dad never batted an eye. "Son," he said, "I will support you one hundred percent. You do what you want to do. Just be sure when you try out that you're always visible. Always be there. Let them know how hungry you are to play."

ASU was a long way from home, but I was too focused to get very homesick. Anyway, I felt as if my family was there with me. My father's advice echoed in my head every day. And the love of my mother—from racing me home every day from elementary school, to getting up in the wee hours to help with my paper route, to working in the cafeteria at Libertyville High and becoming a favorite of my friends—was always with me. Mom was the greatest. I was proud that she got a whole bunch of thank-you notes from my buddies when they graduated from high school. She was the one who would not allow them to steal food by hiding it under their plates or slipping it into their pockets, and yet she didn't make them feel like criminals either. She just made them admit they were stealing it, and then she would buy it for them. Mom opened our house to everyone, and she was as much my friend as my mother.

The first guy I met at Arizona State was Ken Gabriel. He was a little bigger than I was, but we almost looked like twins. We were both left-handed and we could both run. When we discovered we were both walk-ons with high hopes, we became friends and room-mates, and still see each other occasionally today.

If I ever should have been more realistic or even pessimistic about my impossible dream, it should have been when I found out I was one of 209 walk-ons. The varsity baseball team was well stocked with scholarship players—the best all-staters from all over the country and several upperclassmen who were already all-Americans and would wind up in the big leagues.

I didn't get close to Jim Brock. He was busy with the team that was already in place. One of the assistant coaches who helped work out and try out the walk-ons let us know from the beginning that we all had an equal shot, but the odds were against us. "You need to know right off the bat that you've got less than a one in twenty chance of even making the junior varsity here. As long as we're all clear on that, let's get started."

Apparently it wasn't unusual to have a couple of hundred walk-ons at Arizona State, but it was very unusual if even five per-cent of them survived the cuts.

Day after day they looked us over. And every day there was a cut list. Ken Gabriel and I survived the first five cuts, then six, then seven, then eight. We were all over the place, running, diving, throwing, battling each other to be first in the sprints and all the other various drills. Often we were called by each other's names. We would hear coaches saying, "Is that Gabriel?"

"No, that's Butler!"

There would be one more cut. Out of 209 walk-ons, 201 would go away disappointed. Ken and I made it! We were among the final eight. I was thrilled. All I had wanted was a chance to show my stuff.

It was amazing that I could hit anything after so few at bats during my senior year at high school. I hit more in summer ball than I had the entire school season. Somehow, though, I was fresh. Ken and I made that junior varsity team, and I wound up getting a lot of playing time and hitting nearly .340.

I hadn't expected to make the varsity as a freshman, so I wasn't disappointed. Almost every player on that roster wound up drafted and at least half of them spent some time in the major leagues.

I was not the type of hitter then that I am today. Now I'm known as a slap hitter, a bunter, a base-stealing and scoring threat. I had that kind of speed back then and often was able to manufacture runs, but I used a big bat and didn't choke up. I pulled everything to right field and had a big, powerful swing. At the end of the season I approached the JV coach. I said, "Coach, I'm gonna need a scholarship to come back next year."

He looked up at me and shook his head. "I can't do anything for you," he said. "Not as a sophomore. If you have another good year, maybe when you're a junior we can do something. They're cutting baseball scholarships from twenty-eight to thirteen. There's just not enough to go around."

Kenny Landreaux and Bobby Pate were ahead of me at ASU, so I wasn't even sure I'd make varsity as a sophomore. I headed home disappointed but no less determined. Nobody ever said it would be easy.

My next setback came when I got back to Illinois and found that my great year as a freshman on the ASU JV team meant nothing to the coach of the Libertyville entry in the prestigious semi-pro Shoreline League. I was too old for Legion ball and too far ahead of the competition for other leagues designed for my age. The Shoreline was where adults played.

I called Bobby Harju, my acquaintance from the Zion-Benton High School team and told him my predicament. "They don't have room for you on the Libertyville team?" he asked, incredulous.

"That's what they're telling me," I said.

"I'll get right back to you."

Bobby was playing that summer for a legendary Zion team in the Shoreline League, sponsored by the Dill Brothers. The team

no longer exists, but for many years some great players represented that club.

Bobby called his player/coach Gary Bereiter (who now
coaches both baseball and football at Zion-Benton High School).
He told him he knew of a good player who would add something
to their team. Bobby called me back. "Bereiter says you can come
and meet him, and he'll take a look."

That was all I needed to hear. I drove over to Zion and met the
coach. I could tell he was a little shocked at how small and young I
looked. "You graduated from Libertyville?"

"Yes, sir."

"Where'd you play this year?"

"Arizona State."

Bereiter smiled. "Sure you did!"

"Yeah," I said. "I really did. JV. Hit .340. I need to play this
summer."

I won the starting job in center field and hit a ton for that
team. In fact, though I was one of the youngest (and certainly the
smallest) players in the Shoreline League, I won the batting crown
with a .507 average. Interestingly, Bobby Harju hit in the high
.400's himself, and we traded places at the top of the batting race
all summer.

I spent a lot of time with Bobby during those months. We
played mostly night games, and often I spent the night at his
house. He remembers I kept him up all hours talking about my
dream of playing in the major leagues. He wanted to play pro ball
too, and I often got on his case when people would ask him what
his future plans were and he would vacillate between baseball or
something "more realistic." I would say, "C'mon, Bobby, you
want to be a big leaguer just like me, don't you?"

He says I told him one night that I prayed every day that I'd
get a chance to play in the big leagues. "I just have to," I told him.

One of Bobby's favorite stories is that we were jogging out to
our positions between innings one time and we were playfully rag-

ging each other about who would win the batting crown. He was saying something about being ahead of me by a few points and I was saying, "Yeah, just wait and see who's on top at the end of the year."

Bobby stopped at shortstop, and when I was halfway out to center I turned and got in one last lick. "In a few years, *I'll* be playing pro baseball!"

He says I had a little smile that made him laugh. But then, Bobby recalls, he glanced out at me while we outfielders were throwing warm-up tosses to each other, and he noticed my huge smile. He caught my eye, and while I don't remember this as well as he does, he claims I said, "You know I will be, don't you?!"

From that point on, Bobby never doubted my resolve or my chances. He's been as thrilled for me as anyone, but he was one of the least surprised.

The home diamond for Dill Brothers was at the Zion Park District. There was no home run fence, but deep right field was a little stream full of ducks and deep left-center field had picnic tables, which were nearly unreachable by the hitters. Well, somebody almost reached them. I was way back in center when a power hitter cracked one deep to my right. I ran a long way and dove at the last minute, snagging the ball and sliding under those picnic tables. Bobby had headed out to take the relay, assuming the ball would get past us outfielders, and when he saw me lying there under the table, he just kept coming. He thought for sure I'd killed myself. By the time I got up, Bobby and both the other outfielders ran back in with me. It sure seemed a long way.

I had fun hitting balls into that stream *in deep right*. A shot in there on the fly was a homer, on a roll it was a triple. I had a lot of both that summer. It was one of the most fun seasons I had before the majors.

That summer I hit well and had a few outstanding games against Lake Forest. Then I had to face their big fastball pitcher named Bob Olufs. He struck me out two or three times that game, though I might have scratched out a hit off him. After the game he asked to talk to our center fielder. I shook hands with him. "Are you the one leading the league in hitting?"

I nodded.

"I think I might be able to get you a scholarship to Southeastern Oklahoma State."

I had never heard of that school, and I couldn't imagine going to a small town in the middle of nowhere. But that word *scholarship* got my attention. "I'm listening."

"And by the way," Bob said, "who's that little lead-off hitter for you guys?"

I looked close to see if he was kidding. He wasn't. "Bob, that's me."

I watched for signs that he regretted promising to put in a good word for me with his coach when he realized I was the little lead-off man he had struck out two or three times that game. He called his coach, but for a long time I heard nothing.

I had no preconceived notions when I finally accepted an invitation from the Southeastern Oklahoma coach, Don (Doc) Parham, to visit him in Durant, Oklahoma, for a look-see. I was a big-city kid, raised in L.A. and Chicago, now flying to Dallas/Ft. Worth and then being driven to Podunk, USA. Well, if nothing else, at least I'd have a chance to show somebody what I could do.

Doc Parham recalls his first impressions of me:

"My All-American pitcher, Bob Olufs, called me one day and said there was an outfielder playing in his summer league in the Chicago area who had been to Arizona State a year and wasn't sure he wanted to go back. He said we might be able to get him. My immediate reaction was, 'Bob, we don't need another outfielder. We're in good shape.' And we were. We had three great outfielders, all with good bats, good speed, and good arms.

"Bob had sounded so impressed with this kid, though, that

after a week of thinking about it I called him back. I said, 'Bob, maybe we ought to look at that guy.'

"Bob told me, 'I think he's decided to go back to Arizona State.'

"I said, 'At least get him to come down here so I can take a look.'

"Brett was still pretty sure he was going back to ASU, but for some reason he came down. I had someone pick him up at D/FW and drive him the ninety or so miles to our campus. I was in my office, which faces University Boulevard, and when they pulled in across the road and that little guy got out and started across the street, the first thing that struck me was, *This guy is not too big.*

"When he came into the office and I stood to greet him, I was looking down on him. I was saying to myself, 'Bob, what have you got me into here?'

"We visited a while, and I liked him. He was a good-natured, friendly kid who loved to talk baseball. I said, 'Come on up to the ball field and let me see you swing a little in the cage.'

"He stepped in there, and I turned on the machine, and oh, he looked awful. He must have swung and missed at fifteen straight pitches. If you ask me now what I saw in him, I couldn't tell you. But there was something there. Even without his making contact with the ball, I liked him. He looked like a ballplayer. He was small, but he carried himself well and made some kind of impression on me."

After my less-than-impressive session in the cage, Doc and I went back to his office and talked a little more. I was stunned when he offered me a scholarship. I couldn't remember having looked so bad at the plate, but Doc kept saying he understood there was a lot of pressure on a guy trying out for a coach. He said he'd seen that a lot of times, especially with guys facing machines they weren't used to. He told me he could get me a partial scholarship, and if I showed well in the preseason he could make it a full ride. I didn't accept on the spot, but he sure gave me a lot to think about.

When I got back to Libertyville, of course, Mom and Dad wanted to hear all about it. "So what did you think?" they asked.

"It was nice," I said. "And I liked the coach. But I think I'm going back to Arizona State."

Somehow, that decision gave me no peace. I talked to my parents a lot about it, but they reminded me the choice was mine. My dad also reminded me that after my sophomore year, I was on my own financially. The scholarship at ASU was certainly not guaranteed, and probably not likely. I was having trouble sleeping, worrying and praying about what to do. One night, about two o'clock in the morning, I got up to get something to drink. When I turned the light on in the kitchen I was startled to see my mother standing there. I just looked at her and shook my head.

"You've got to go to Oklahoma, don't you?"

"Yeah, Mom. I don't know why, but God has put this in my life for some reason."

The decision had been made.

Doc Parham immediately became like a second father to me. He had told me straight out that he already had his three starting outfielders, but I had a chance to compete for a job. That's all I wanted.

During the preseason, I hit about .620. I was jerking home runs 450 feet to right field, over the fence, past the tennis courts, and up a little hill to the base of a dormitory. Doc couldn't believe a little guy could generate such power, and now he finds it hard to believe that I'm a slap hitter in the majors.

I probably still would have been the fourth outfielder on that team, but one of the guys got into academic trouble, and all of a sudden I was a starter on a university varsity baseball team on a full scholarship.

My uniform number? Two, of course.

There's no telling what I might have done at Arizona State

University. Who knows, they might not have even given me a chance. It's interesting—if you look in the trophy case at ASU today, you'll see me pictured with the alumni who went on to the major leagues. But the first time someone mentioned me to Jim Brock after I made the majors, he said that if I had gone to ASU, he'd have known about it. Later he amended that to imply that I had been an unimpressive freshman walk-on.

What I had told my mother about going to Oklahoma was right. I believe God had put this together. I was in the right place at the right time, and apparently I was ready. My first spring there, as a sophomore in 1977, we were 56-8. I hit .388. We went to the NAIA World Series in St. Joseph, Missouri, and lost to David Lipscomb in the finals.

The next year was one of my best ever. I became the first .400 hitter in the history of the school, with a .439 average. My last year I hit .364 for a three-year average of .394. I was named all-American twice and All-National Tournament Team twice. I played on the U.S. National Team that toured South Korea and Taiwan. In the 176 games I played at Southeastern, we won 146, for a winning percentage of .830.

Southeast Oklahoma State University, Durant, Oklahoma
Brett Butler

YR	G	AB	R	H	E	2B	3B	HR	SB	SAC	HP	BB	K	RBI	AVG.
1977	64	209	67	81	1	12	4	11	22	3	2	56	34	56	.388
1978	50	155	62	68	4	10	5	10	13	4	0	48	14	55	.439
1979	62	195	80	71	4	7	6	10	21	1	2	58	19	49	.364
TOTAL	176	559	209	220	9	29	15	31	56	8	4	162	67	160	.394

My thirty-one career homers were a record at that time, and Doc has always been generous with his comments about my days playing under him. He has told people, "Brett was an intense competitor. He didn't like to lose. He never missed practice. He didn't drink. He didn't smoke. He just didn't do things that hurt you. That's why he's still playing center field at his age.''

During my junior year we had a second baseman, Ronnie Gooch, who was one of the best players I ever played with. He expected to go in the first round of the major-league draft. I had a great .439 average year and fully expected to be drafted too. Gooch was picked in the fifteenth round. I was ignored. And I was crushed.

When I got the word, I just wanted to be by myself. I asked, *Why, Lord?* but I knew I had to put negative thinking behind me. I prayed, *I'm just going to trust that you know what's going on and you know what's in store.*

No matter what, I would not be dissuaded from my dream.

ALMOST
THERE

The Philadelphia Phillies invited me to a weeklong camp after my junior year at Southeastern Oklahoma State. They liked me and invited me back the next week because they wanted a top major-league scout to evaluate me. I felt I showed well for him, too, and they told me I was impressive. Yet when all the rounds of the draft had been announced, my name was not there.

Doc felt almost as bad for me as I felt for myself. He remembers: "Brett was such an intense competitor. He wanted to be first in everything. The other guys used to joke about the way he carried a stat sheet around in his back pocket. I'm sure some of them even resented the drive he had, but it wasn't anything negative directed toward anybody else. He just wanted to be the best. And in most categories, he was. Besides always looking like a ballplayer, he had a great attitude. He was clean as a whistle. There was never a personality problem, and I knew he'd be the last guy who would let a ball fall when he could get to it. He was a coach's player.

"The only time he missed practice, and I didn't know about it until recently, he had made himself sick trying to chew tobacco.

He didn't tell me, but he came to practice and got sick and had to go back to the dorm. I think that was the worst thing he'd ever done. He was a great competitor, a great kid to be around."

Somehow, and again I trace this back to the outlook of my parents, I was able to put my shock and disappointment behind me and stay at the task of making the big leagues. My dream nearly consumed me, but even back then my life consisted of more than baseball. For one thing, since shortly after I had arrived on campus, I was in love.

The girl was a senior at Durant High School near the Southeastern campus. My roommate dated her best friend, and her father was a friend of Doc Parham. Patty (not her real name) was probably enamored with me at first because I was two years older and a college student. I was her first love, and I believed I loved her too. Of course, I didn't really know what love was until I met Eveline, but Patty and I dated for several years and we were engaged before I graduated.

Maybe I just wasn't paying attention, but I thought Patty was as thrilled as I was when I finally got word at the end of my senior season that Doc Parham had good news for me.

"You've been drafted by the Atlanta Braves," he said. It was almost anticlimactic. I had been waiting so long, I didn't know what to say.

"Doc, what does that mean? What round?"

"Twenty-third round," he said. I wondered how many hundreds of ballplayers had been drafted before me. I knew the odds, even for those who were signed, were a hundred-to-one against them ever appearing in a major-league game. The odds against me must have been ten-thousand-to-one.

"What happens now?" I asked.

"The Atlanta scout, Bob Mavis, is going to meet you at a hotel on the outskirts of Durant. He has a contract for you and he'll tell you where to report."

When I shook hands with Bob Mavis, he smiled and said,

"Congratulations, Brett, and welcome to the Atlanta Braves organization. I wish you all the best."

We sat down and he handed me a contract. I pretended to know what I was reading, studying it and basically just looking for my signing bonus. Of course, there's not much of a bonus for someone signed in the lower rounds, especially the twenty-third. When I saw the figure, one thousand dollars, I looked up quickly. "Mr. Mavis, this isn't gonna do it. I need at least five thousand. I have nothing. I need a car."

Mavis stood and began gathering up the documents. "Brett," he said, "I wasn't going to tell you this, but the thousand you would get by signing this contract is coming out of my own pocket. Your being drafted at all was a favor to your coach."

I could have let that truth slam me up against the wall and knock the wind out of me, but I was concentrating too much on not letting Bob Mavis get away. "Just tell me where to sign, sir," I said. No way he was getting out of that hotel with my pro contract. It was June, 1979, and I didn't care whether it was a favor to my coach or not. I was now a professional baseball player. The big leagues were still a long way off, but I knew there was no getting there without this first step.

Was my selection by the Atlanta Braves really just a favor to Doc? Yes. He confirmed it later. Doc says: "Did I think Brett was going to be a big leaguer? No. But I thought he deserved to be drafted. He was as good a player as I ever coached, and though he may not have hit me or anyone else at first glance as an obvious big-league prospect, I talked him up to a lot of scouts. One from Kansas City told me that every time he came to scout someone else, Brett would hit a home run. I said, 'Then why don't you draft him?' 'I'll tell you what, coach,' he said, 'if he hits one over the tennis courts today, I will sign him.'

"Brett hit one over the tennis courts that day, but that guy still didn't sign him. He said 'Doc, I just can't. He's too little.'

"I'm sure it was his lack of height that scared most of them off.

But they were wrong. He was very nearly a five-point player. He could run, he could hit, he could hit for power, he could field, and he had a fair arm. He'd never been a real strong-armed center fielder, but he's always been very accurate. But scouts told me they were afraid artificial turf hits would bounce over his head. He's long since proved them wrong on that. He's one of the smartest players in the big leagues. He knows where to position himself and how to track a ball.

"Yes, I pleaded with Bob Mavis to draft him as a favor to me. We've been friends for years. I told him, 'Just give Brett a chance. Let him get his foot in the door and he'll do the rest. If he doesn't perform, then that'll be the end of it.' "

I didn't know all that back then, of course, but my attitude was, just let me in there. Tell me I'm too little, too weak. Okay, fine. Just give me a chance and I'll prove I can play.

Patty and I were both upset that I would be heading toward Atlanta for instructional ball, but I thought we were both upset about the same thing. I would miss her and I assumed she would miss me. Actually, it was more than that. We would be apart for about six months, communicating only through letters and phone calls, but my plan was to come back and marry her.

I had always thought it would be fun to be married at home plate, like my teammate Scott Loucks. He had been married before the final game at the NAIA world series. In the game just before that, I had been picked off first base. When I told my father I might like to get married on the field someday, he cracked, "Yeah, but you'd have to have a ceremony about ten feet from first base!"

All the Braves draftees, dozens of us, were sent to Fulton County Stadium in Atlanta. You could see in the eyes of some of the guys that they had never seen that many star players in one place at one time. Their pro careers were finished before they started. They were totally intimidated. Other guys tried to get along on talent alone. They caroused, womanized, drank, and stayed out late. That cost them in their performance. I knew we were all just babies, all trying to get our break. I had to stay healthy, get lucky, and stay prepared so I'd be ready for any opportunity that arose.

While I wanted to be friends and just one of the guys, I also felt a desperate need to be noticed by the coaches. It would be easy to slip through the cracks with that many guys around. So I developed an attitude. I was cocky. I put my batting gloves in my back pockets and walked with a swagger. If people thought I was a preening little rooster, at least they would notice me. I had a flair for catching a fly and flipping it back into the infield. If people smirked and shook their heads, that was all right with me. At least they would remember me and know I could do the job.

My style was a means to an end. Everybody started at this level and then they would be parceled out to various teams at various levels of the minor leagues. Everyone wanted to start out as high as possible and start moving toward that ultimate goal, the majors. I was one of the lowest picks on the team, and just like everyone else, I kept an eye out for the Braves' number one pick, Brad Komminsk. We all wanted to know the same thing: was he worth the big signing money? Everybody compared himself to everyone else. I knew I was seen as a guy starting at the bottom. That suited me and my personality just fine. Without that challenge, I might not have performed. I may have been a natural talent, but because of my size I've always had to work at it. So there are a hundred guys to beat out? All right. I'm gonna be the first one there, I'm going to hustle the most, they're going to see my flamboyancy. Even if they don't want to notice me, they'll have to, because I'll be in their faces. Once I had their attention, I had to perform because if you do all that and then don't come through, they quickly send you packing.

Occasionally the coaches would test us. One would ask, "Brett, do you think you can hit .300 in the big leagues?"

"Yeah."

"Boy, that sounds kind of arrogant."

"Well, I really think I can do it."

"Really?"

"Yeah. Give me a chance. You won't know unless you let me try."

That's how I was. If I didn't believe I could do it, I wouldn't have been there. My father had always told me, "If you can back it up, it's confidence, not arrogance." I'm sure my act wore a little thin on people, but in the end, it worked.

The path to the big leagues in the Atlanta organization started in Bradenton for what seemed to be the youngest players. Next up the ladder was Kingsport, then Greenwood, then Savannah, then Richmond, and then the big leagues. When I was assigned to Bradenton, I was mad. I don't know why I expected to start anywhere but right at the bottom, but I wondered why I was going down there with all those kids just out of high school. Heck, I was a college graduate. Again though, I got over it quickly and decided to add it to my motivational fuel. If they thought I belonged in Bradenton, I'd show them quickly that I was ready for Greenwood. In just thirty games in Bradenton, I put up numbers similar to those I had achieved at Southeastern Oklahoma State. I hit .369 and was then assigned to Greenwood. There I hit over .300 and fully expected to be promoted to Savannah the next season. Patty and I were still on course to be married in about a year if everything went as expected. We saw each other infrequently, of course, and I was gone for long stretches at a time. I looked forward to the day when she would be with me, and I assumed she was thinking the same way.

The next season, 1980, the Braves dropped the Kingsport team and added Anderson and Durham as the two steps before Savannah and Richmond and then the big leagues in Atlanta. Bradenton was still rookie ball, Anderson was low A ball, Durham was high Class A, Savannah was Class AA, and Richmond was Class

AAA. During spring training, I was assigned to work out with the Savannah club, and I was fired up. I was convinced I was going to make that team. After spring training all the minor leaguers met in one room and the rosters were read off. First they made the assignments to Savannah. I was not on that roster. That was okay, I knew I was going to Durham. But when they read off the Durham roster, I wasn't on that either. I was mad. I had been assigned to Anderson. I was still in low A ball. As soon as the meeting was over I walked into Hank Aaron's office. As a lifetime baseball fan, I had put Hank Aaron on a pedestal. I still believe he was one of the greatest to ever play the game. But that didn't keep me from speaking my mind. I was almost twenty-three years old and could have jeopardized my whole big-league career, but I gave him both barrels.

"I can't believe you're sending me to Anderson," I said. "I've been working out with Savannah, and I've been hitting well and running well."

Hank tried to calm me down. "Now, Brett, you know as well as I do that you can get to Savannah just as easily from Anderson as you can from Durham."

I said, "No, I can see what's happening here. I thought you sent the best talent up there. You're going to send one of your favorites ahead of me, even though I deserve it."

Hank looked puzzled. "Brett, you do your job and you'll have the same chance as anyone else."

I came as close to quitting as I ever had. I went grudgingly to Anderson and told my manager down there, Sonny Jackson, that I couldn't stand what they were doing to me. Sonny's a sweet guy and I love him dearly. He said, "Hey, Brett, prove them wrong." Sonny was right. I just needed a little more negative motivation. I did well, and halfway through the season I was promoted to Durham. I hit over .365 there and we made the play-offs.

Hank Aaron came down to see one of the games. He called me

over. "Brett," he said, "we finally got you where you're supposed to be."

I said, "No you didn't. I should be in Savannah." And I walked away. It may not have been the smartest career move, but I was cocky. My feeling was, If I don't make it with the Braves I'm gonna make it with somebody. But you're not going to hold me down. I'm going to prosper.

At the end of the 1980 season I went down to the Florida instructional league and played for Eddie Haas. Milt Thompson, who would become a big leaguer and who was the one I thought Hank Aaron favored over me, was on that team too. Milt led off and played center. I hit in the two hole and played left. For a long stretch, Milt was hitting about .200 and I was hitting about .400, so Eddie decided to have me lead off. The next thing we knew, the Atlanta brass was on its way down to watch us play. The owner, Ted Turner, Bobby Cox, Hank Aaron, and Pat Nugent would all be there.

Before the game, Hank told Eddie to put Milt in center field and have him lead off. He said, "Butler's been playing, hasn't he?"

"Yeah."

"Then sit him down. Rest him today."

Here was my big chance to show what I could do in front of the guys who make all the decisions, and I would be sitting. I was mad and I didn't understand it, but I didn't have to stay frustrated long.

Bobby Cox, who was not aware of what Hank had said to Eddie, came over and said, "I've heard about this kid Butler. How come he's not playing? Put him in there. I want to see him play."

That was all I needed. I feel everyone gets at least one break on his way to the big leagues, and when it happens, you'd better not fail. This was my opportunity to show them I could play. In the next four games I got twelve hits.

Preparation had met opportunity, and before we disbanded

for the year, I was told I would be invited to spring training with the big league club. I had finished the 1980 season in Class A ball at Durham, and now I would have a shot at making the majors. I couldn't wait. My future looked bright, and I decided it was time to get married.

Patty and I hadn't seen each other for six months. When I went back to Oklahoma intending to marry her, something was different. I felt as if I had been drawn into a routine. She was cordial, but nothing more. I said, "Hey, I haven't seen you in six months. What's up?"

Finally, she gave me an ultimatum. "Brett, you're going to have to make a decision. You have to choose between me or baseball."

"Wow." I sighed and sat down. "If you love me, you know how much baseball means to me. I love you and you'll always have a place in my heart, but I've got to play ball."

She told me her parents would give us a dry cleaner franchise in their chain and that we could stay right there in Oklahoma. That would have been about last on my list of things I wanted to do.

"You know I've just got to try to do this baseball thing," I said. "I'm so close."

I went back to Illinois to visit my family for Thanksgiving and then went back to Oklahoma to give Patty one more chance at Christmas. She had not changed her mind. Neither had I. I headed back to Illinois to wait for spring training.

I was not proud of the physical relationship we had had over the past several years. I knew that as a Christian I couldn't justify it. God had helped sift out so many bad habits in my life, but I had hung on to that one. One day I knelt in my room and prayed, *Lord, I ask you to forgive me for rationalizing and justifying and manipulating Patty into doing what I wanted. I'm tired of living a hypocritical life. Please put a godly woman in my life to take the desires of the flesh away from me. I want someone I can love for the rest of my life. And I want to become a bond slave to you.*

I had a great spring in 1981. Just like at Arizona State University with all those walk-ons, I kept surviving the daily cuts. By opening day, Bobby Cox had to have the ball club down to twenty-four players. On the last day of camp, he called me in. He congratulated me on a great spring and said he'd like to keep me. My heart sank. "I'd like to," he repeated, "but they won't let me."

I said, "Bobby, come on! You need a lead-off guy."

He said, "No, the time isn't right. You go down and have a good year. You'll be back here soon enough."

"Aw, Bobby. Where am I going?"

"Richmond."

I had almost made the big leagues. I had almost gone from Class A to the majors in one season. Well, going from Class A to Class AAA wasn't that bad either. I felt closer to God than I ever had. I remember praying *Lord, you know how much I want to be in the big leagues, but obviously you have a reason for this.*

I had been so close to the majors I could smell it and taste it. I was determined to do whatever I needed in Richmond to earn my way back to Atlanta.

Eddie Haas was managing Richmond, so I looked forward to playing for him. My first day there, I showed up with all my sweatbands, a turtleneck, gloves hanging out the back—still sporting my attitude. Eddie said, "Butler, what are you doing? Take that crap off. If I see it again, I'm going to send you to AA."

I didn't have to be told twice. I wanted my next stop to be up, not down. I may have been cocky, but I was coachable. I was willing to do whatever it took to make it.

EIGHT

EVELINE

Knowing I was on the threshold of a major-league career made me more serious about trying to get my spiritual house in order. I had told God I wanted to be his bond servant. I knew from the Old Testament that a bond servant was a slave who had chosen to stay with his master. My master was Christ. He had seemed to sift my life until the cussing and the drinking and the temper were pretty much under control. Though I had a reputation among my teammates as a bit of a skirt chaser, my plan was to change my ways.

I believe God choreographs the steps of his children. There's not a doubt in my mind that God knew exactly where I would be in the spring of 1981 and that it would just happen to be where I met the love and soul mate of my life.

While I was in Oklahoma, deciding against Patty's ultimatum, a beautiful young coed I had never met was attending a Christmas pageant in Richmond, Virginia, which would change her life forever.

A couple of months later I was in Florida with the Braves for spring training, trying to make the big-league club. I was unaware that during a game in West Palm Beach my future wife was in the stands with her college girlfriends. She noticed a Brave step up to the plate with the number 62 on his back. She turned to her friends with a laugh. "Look at that shrimpo! He'll never make it."

But I did, of course.

A few weeks later the Braves broke camp. I was the last player cut, but I was headed to Richmond, which I truly believed would be my last stop before Atlanta and the big leagues. Once we settled into our apartments on April 1, 1981, we decided to thank the college girls who had made the housing arrangements by taking them out for dinner at a Ruby Tuesday. There were about fifteen guys and five girls, and I noticed one right away, taken with her eyes and her smile. I asked a friend, "Who's the blonde?"

"That's my girl, Eveline," he said.

I didn't think much more about it until I ran into Eveline a couple of weeks later at a disco. My friend was nowhere to be seen. I said, "I thought you had a date tonight."

She said, "A date? I don't have a date."

I told her my friend had said he was going out with his girl-friend. She said, "Well, he doesn't date me. He dates my room-mate."

I said, "No he doesn't. He dates you!"

Eveline said, "I think I know who I date."

That's when I realized that my friend had told me he was dating Eveline only because he knew she was a nice girl and he wanted to protect her from a guy with a reputation like mine.

"Well, then, do you want to go out?" I asked.

"No," Eveline said.

"Why not?"

"I know you baseball players. You're all the same."

"Do you mind if I sit with you and your friends?"

"Well, the table's kind of full."

Their table was set up against a railing, which separated them from the dance floor. I picked up a chair and went onto the dance floor, excusing myself and moving people out of the way. I put the chair on the other side of the railing, and said, "Hi! How you guys doin'?"

Eveline thought I was weird. Like an idiot, I pulled out pictures of my former fiancée. Eveline told her girlfriends, "Stay away from this guy. He's on the rebound."

Eveline remembers what happened next: "He asked me to dance, and I didn't see any harm in that. On the noisy, crowded dance floor, however, he said, 'Have you seen the Gator?'

"I could barely hear him. I said 'What?'

" 'HAVE YOU SEEN THE GATOR?'

" 'No, what are you talking about?'

"With that, he literally dropped to the dance floor on his stomach and moved his arms and legs like an alligator. Everybody was staring at him and then at me. 'You're a jerk!' I said, and just walked off. I was mortified. First this guy was pulling out pictures of his old girlfriend and now he's on the floor acting like an alligator!

"I was so embarrassed I hurried away to get something to drink. Pretty soon he walked up behind me."

I was trying to impress Eveline, but it seemed she really didn't like me. My whole life was a challenge, so I wasn't about to give up easily. "Will you go out with me?" I asked.

"No," she said. "I already told you I won't go out with you."

"Come on," I said. "What will it hurt? Do you like Italian food?"

"Well, yeah."

"We'll go out for Italian food."

"No."

"Do you like to bowl?"

"Yeah."

"Then we'll go out for Italian food and we'll go bowling. What harm can that do?"

"Okay, all right! If I go out with you one time will you promise to leave me alone?"

"Yeah, but if you go out with me once, you'll probably end up marrying me."

Eveline was nearly gagging.

She says: "It was the worst approach ever. This guy was so cocky, he thought he hung the moon. He was totally not the type of a guy I dated. I could have gotten rid of him and probably should have, but I didn't think one date would do any harm and I knew I wouldn't let this thing progress."

I had told my friends to leave without me, so when it was time to go, Eveline said, "Where are your friends?"

"Oh," I said, "they left."

"How are you getting home?"

"I'm gonna walk."

Well, Eveline was the one who had arranged for the apartments where we were staying, so she knew how far away they were—seven or eight miles. There was no way she would let me walk. She said, "I'll take you home. Get in the car."

I said, "Oh no, no. That's okay. I'll walk."

But she insisted. What could I do? I had no choice. I accepted.

Eveline remembers: "So I drove him home, and he got out in front of the apartment. Then he leaned back in and said, 'Do you want to come in?'

"I said, 'No! Just shut the door!' "

When I shut the door, she leaned over and locked it. I thought, *What is her problem?*

I was the problem, Eveline says.

A few days later I called her. "You said you wanted to go out."

Eveline remembers that we had a great time. "We had Italian food and we went bowling. I found Brett talkative and very funny. He was also kind. He talked a lot about his family, about how special they were and how much he loved his brother and his little sister and how he always felt he had to take care of her. Of course he talked about baseball too and how he was going to make the major leagues. I said, 'That's great that you have all that confidence.' Regardless of how obnoxious he might have been initially, I saw in him what I wanted for myself in terms of self-confidence. He had direction and purpose. I thought, *Wow, how great to have things straightened out.*

"When he told me he was a Christian, I said, 'Well, that's really neat.'

"He told me how he had prayed to receive Christ at a Fellowship of Christian Athletes conference when he was in high school. 'I just became a Christian in December,' I told him.

"He was thrilled for me, but we didn't get into any big discussions about God that night."

After dinner Eveline and I went bowling. We bet a house on the game. She was a great bowler. She thought she was going to beat me because she grew up bowling. I beat her, but not by much. She said, "Okay, you win. I'll buy you a house someday."

Eveline remembers that I didn't call for a few days, but she says, "I had to admit to myself that I really liked this guy. He was sweet. When he finally called, I didn't want to act anxious. He asked if I wanted to go with him to a team party the next day. I said, 'You know, I've got a lot going on. Let me check my calendar.' I put my hand over the phone and just waited a few moments. Then I came back on. 'I think I have some time free in the afternoon.' "

Eveline and I had a great time chitchatting on that second date. I don't know where we went on our third date, but at the end of the evening I took her back to the apartment I shared with a couple of teammates. I sat her down on the couch and I blurted, "You're gonna think I'm the craziest person in the world, but I believe God put you in my life. I want you to ask me any question you want to and I'll answer it truthfully to the best of my ability. Anything you want to know about me."

Eveline's first question was characteristically direct. "How many women have you slept with?"

We joke that it took several hours for me to go down the list, but of course that isn't true. I was not proud of my past, but I had some scruples. I was never a one-night-stand type of a guy. I knew I had rationalized and justified sin, but I also knew I wasn't as base as some guys are.

I wanted to know everything about this girl. As soon as she started telling me her story, I was mesmerized and captivated. By the end of the evening we were both crying. She told me she was saying things she had never told another soul. Eveline had just finished her junior year at Virginia Commonwealth University in Richmond and had come to that point in her life where she knew she needed a change.

She had grown up in Vienna, Virginia, near Washington, D.C., the youngest of three kids and the only girl. "My parents' marriage was a disaster," she said. "When I was seven, my mother divorced my father and moved all three kids to an apartment. My parents' love was conditional. I was constantly told I would never amount to anything, that I was worthless. I had no reason to believe otherwise. When my mother remarried, she soon found out her new husband was not what he appeared. He wouldn't give her a divorce, so while my brothers and I were at school one day, my mother moved out of the house and changed the locks. Our family lived with friends for three months until my mother was able to get the divorce and move us back home."

Though I had dated Eveline only three times, I felt protective of her. Her story broke my heart. She said, "We never went to church, but I always wanted to. I often begged my friends' parents to take me, and for a while I attended a Catholic church. Someone invited me to a children's club meeting at a Baptist church where the program included memorizing Scripture verses. One that stayed with me for years was, 'Except a man be born again, he cannot enter the Kingdom of God.'

"I had deep thoughts about God for as long as I could remember. When I was eleven I sat praying on a hillside near my home. One of my brothers told me I would live and I would die and that would be the end of it. I didn't want to believe that. I didn't believe it. I asked God, *Who am I? Why am I here? Where am I going?*

"The next time my mother married, I enjoyed a normal family life for the first time. I also inherited another older brother when my father remarried. He and I are still close . My stepdad taught me to play tennis, and I was also into gymnastics and cheerleading. I was active in lots of stuff in high school, but I never felt comfortable. I never quite fit in. I was loud and boisterous, cynical and negative. I trusted very few people.

"A school friend, Lisa Ingram, often talked to me about God. Though part of me longed to know him, another part of me didn't want to have anything to do with God. I wondered, *If my life is so miserable and I'm so unhappy, how could God really care about me? If God loved me, wouldn't my life be wonderful?*

"When I was a junior in high school, my stepfather died suddenly of a heart attack and I wondered what else could go wrong in my life. I was involved in an abusive relationship and didn't know how to get out of it. My consuming passion was to get through high school and get away from home."

What Eveline told me about her high school boyfriend made me want to kill him, but even more, I just wanted to protect her from any future pain. She told me that with all she went through, she slid into a deep depression and virtually quit eating. "Between my junior and senior years," she said, "I lost 47 pounds. I'm only 5'1", but I went from 128 pounds to 89 pounds in just a few months.

"I saw something in Lisa that I didn't have and I wanted it. But I never felt worthy enough. One day Lisa brought me an article she had found about a disease called anorexia nervosa. She said,

'Eveline, I want you to read this. I really think you have this disease.'

"I told her, 'I don't have anorexia. You're just mad because I'm skinnier than you are.'

"Actually, I knew I was in trouble. I also knew anorexia had nothing to do with food. It had to do with power. My life was out of control. I couldn't control my parents, couldn't control things at school, couldn't control my boyfriend. The only thing I could control was what I put into my mouth. I became weak and got the Hong Kong flu and had a lot of the other side effects of anorexia."

"Did you ever get counseling?" I asked her, fighting tears.

"Just once," she said. "He told me, 'What you really need is to take a hard look at your life and decide that you have value. If you have value, then what you do from here is up to you. Eating or not eating is a by-product of how you feel about yourself. You need to learn to love yourself before anyone else is going to love you. It's in your hands. You can start to take care of yourself and get better.' "

"And did you?" I asked.

"In a sense, I did," she said. "I had already been working for several years in women's fashion. I looked for a college where I could major in distributive education. That's how I found Virginia Commonwealth."

"You seem healthy now," I said.

"Just being out on my own helped turn my life around. I got away from home, away from that guy, and I started making my own decisions. I started working with the VCU basketball program, keeping stats and working in the office. I got a full scholarship to work in the athletic office and should have been happier than ever."

"But?" I said.

"But something was missing. One of the first people I had met in college was a guy who invited me to hear him play his guitar and sing at the Baptist Student Union. I had a lot of questions for him and his friends, questions about God. They told me I needed to receive Christ, but I was convinced God could never love me. The only love I had ever known was based on my own performance, and I always fell short. I didn't have to be convinced I was a sinner. I felt so sinful I doubted God could ever forgive me."

"When did you find out that he would?"

"Well, every Sunday I attended a large denominational church. But I didn't get any answers there about a personal relationship with God, and I got tired of the rituals. I wondered, Where's their commitment? What are they really learning?

"When my friends from the Baptist Student Union told me God loved me unconditionally, I just knew they wouldn't say that if they knew my whole past. But one of them told me, 'When Christ went to the cross and died, he died for you. When they were nailing him to the cross, they were nailing all our sins, not just the sins in our past but every sin we'll ever commit.' That was too much to comprehend.

"But then last December 22, they invited me to the Christmas program at their church. This one was different. It told Christ's whole story, not just his birth. After the nativity scenes, they showed Jesus as an adult, carrying the cross and then dying for the sins of the world. Finally, I understood what it was all about. I knew God loved me and had sent Christ to die for me. I was no more or less worthy than anyone else to receive him. One of the ministers ended the program by saying, 'Before you leave here tonight, you need to know that if you die you're going somewhere. It's either heaven or hell. The choice is yours. No one else will choose for you.'

"There was an invitation for people to come forward and pray to receive Christ, but I didn't dare stand up in front of people. That night I prayed in bed, God, if you are who you say you are in the Bible, I want you to come into my life and change me. I slept soundly that night."

Her story of coming to Christ was so much like mine, it was eerie. But what she said next really hit me. "That's when I started praying that God would put a man in my life who was godly, who I could love, and who would be a spiritual leader for me."

As I listened to Eveline's story, I could hardly believe it. I was already deeply in love with her, and it hurt me so bad to know how she had gone through so much and was so wounded. I knew I was going to marry this girl and that she would be mine for the rest of my life. I felt so protective and had such a sense of ownership already, I gathered her in my arms.

"Eveline," I said, "I'll never let anybody hurt you again."

Eveline remembers that she suddenly felt safe for the first time in her life. "A woman knows when a man is saying something just to make a good impression," she says. "She also knows when a man truly believes and means what he says. I knew Brett meant it. I barely knew him, and yet I felt I knew him better than I had ever known anybody else."

IS THAT
ALL THERE IS?

By now you know I'm not one to whitewash my past. I believe the truth will never hurt you. So I feel compelled to tell you of a season of my life that I'm not proud of.

I had been raised in a godly home and had been a born-again Christian since 1973. I knew God had been doing a real work of sifting in my life, especially during the last several months. I also knew that Eveline was a direct answer to my prayer for a godly woman, and she believed I was the answer to her prayer.

After that third date, we were deeply in love and never looked back. Here, finally, was my chance to stop the rationalizing, the justifying, the selfish manipulating. I was in the most exciting period of my life, excelling in Class AAA baseball, being groomed to become leadoff for the Atlanta Braves, and finally finding out what true love was really all about. The baseball season was in full swing, and I was leading the league in hitting. Wade Boggs (who would become a superstar for the Red Sox and the Yankees) and I battled for the batting title all year.

During that first month of the season, Eveline became my inspiration, the reason to look forward to getting back from a road trip, someone to share all my hopes and dreams.

As the end of the college year rolled around that spring of 1981, Eveline had a crisis of ethical and moral conscience about some of the activities in the office where she worked. She went to her boss and spoke her mind. He said if she wanted to keep her scholarship, she should mind her own business and do her job. She took the high road. Knowing she couldn't afford her senior year without a full-time job and financial help, she still walked away from that scholarship. Her plan was to move back to northern Virginia.

I panicked. "You can't leave me," I said. "No way I want you two-and-a-half hours away. It's bad enough when we're apart on road trips."

"Brett," she said, "I don't know what else to do."

Without thinking, without so much as a conscious memory of having recently told God I was tired of living a hypocritical life, I said, "Move in with me!"

From a practical standpoint, in the eyes of the world, it made perfect sense. I had two roommates who would give us our space, and we told ourselves that necessity was the mother of invention.

We were young and stupid and in love. This time this really was the girl I was going to marry. Just like countless other couples who justify their sin, we decided we were already married in the eyes of God—so who needed a piece of paper to make it official?

Sad to say, we didn't even suffer pangs of guilt. Living together was so common, and we were living through such an exciting period of our lives, we didn't give it a second thought. I was so good at pushing any conflict over this arrangement to the back of my mind that I continued to pray and read my Bible and even tell other people about Christ. Isn't that just the way of the world, justifying sin in our lives to fit our own agenda, not God's?

Eveline and I read the Bible and prayed together frequently. We attended the team Bible studies and I showed up at the baseball chapel meetings. Our relationship was so beautiful, we actually believed we had God's full blessing. He had given Eveline to me and he had given me to her.

We did not, of course, have the blessing of our parents. Mine were disappointed and wanted us to get married and "make it legal." Her parents were very upset. In fact, her father had a very difficult time letting his only daughter make a life-changing decision, for fear she would be hurt. It was Eveline and me against the world, and, at the time, we loved every minute of it.

I had a great season for Richmond, playing under Eddie Haas. He taught me so much. In 125 games I hit .335 and lost the batting title to Wade Boggs by just half a point. I was named the league's Most Valuable Player.

After the game on August 19, 1981, Eveline and my roommates and I had a team party until about four o'clock in the morning. I was sound asleep at seven when the phone rang. It was Richard Anderson, the Richmond general manager. I answered groggily, but the news woke me up instantly. "Brett, you need to be in Atlanta by this afternoon, ready to play tonight."

"What? Are you serious? Really?"

I had strained an ankle recently, but that didn't keep me from jumping all over the apartment, bouncing on the bed, running in place. "I made it!" I shouted. "I finally made it!"

I couldn't keep from laughing and smiling and saying over and over, "I don't know if I can run! I just don't know!"

I called my parents. "Dad, the Braves called me up. I'm going to the show. I made it."

At the airport I was so excited that I just walked through security and didn't look back. When I realized what I had done, I whirled around and ran back to Eveline. " 'Bye! Honey, I love you! I'll call you tonight."

Eveline was crying, partly because she was so happy for me but also because we were going to be apart and we didn't know for how long. I asked her to go to the ballpark and tell Eddie Haas thanks for everything he had done and everything he had taught me. I told her to tell him I hoped I'd see him again.

When she finally got to see Eddie, he said, "I hope I never see him again, because that'll mean he's back down here in the minors."

During the major-league strike earlier that year, some minor-league ballplayers, me included, had been asked to come up to the majors and play in place of the strikers, if it went that far. There was no way I would do that. Why would I cross the players' union? I knew those guys were fighting for my future. Plus, anybody with a brain could see the strike wouldn't last too long. The future of the scabs would be nil.

Ted Turner, the owner of the Braves, knew people still wanted to watch baseball. During the strike, he satisfied their needs by sending a TV crew to Richmond and broadcasting our games into the Atlanta market. So I was not an unknown quantity to Braves fans when I was finally called up. Being so small and looking so young and playing the game with so much exuberance, there had been an immediate love affair with the fans. My name was so similar to that of Rhett Butler of *Gone with the Wind* fame that Atlanta seemed the perfect team for me. I decided I would sign autographs before games and after games until the lights went out.

When I got to Fulton County Stadium for my first major-league game, I was talking to myself. In fact, I talked to myself the whole night. "Do you believe this? Wow! I'm actually here! This is incredible!"

The difference between the major leagues and the minor leagues is huge. In the majors, everything, and I mean everything, is first class. I was rushed up to the front office to sign my contract. Back then, the minimum salary was $32,500. I didn't care. I would have played for nothing. I signed and posed for pictures and shook hands all around, but then someone poked his head in the door and said, "We've got to get Butler downstairs. He's in the starting lineup and he needs to take some BP (batting practice)."

I just about flipped out. I had not expected to be in the lineup. I thought I'd be there a few days and then be called on to pinch hit or pinch run or something. The rest of the team was on the field as I sat in the empty locker room, pulling on the beautiful Braves uniform. I can't believe this, I kept telling myself. This is it. This is the big leagues.

With everything in place, I stopped before a mirror on the way out. My dream had become reality! Yet I was so excited and nervous I didn't know what I might do on the field.

I was so hyper in the batting cage, I pulled most of the BP pitches to right, rather than spraying them around like I should have done. The next thing I knew they were clearing the field so the Mets could hit, and I was playing catch with real big leaguers. Future Hall of Famer Phil "Knucksie" Niekro, the great knuckleballer, was starting for us that night. I was so nervous I prayed I would just be able to hit the ball. During the national anthem I nearly wet my pants. To this day I have to plan ahead, because the national anthem brings on that urge before every game. My hands begin to grow cold as ice and I'm nervous until I finally step into the batter's box.

Of course I can never forget my first at bat in the major leagues, though I have long since forgotten who the pitcher was for the Mets. What had been the most natural thing in the world to me since I was six years old now seemed awkward and stilted. I couldn't get comfortable. My knees were knocking. My heart was racing a hundred miles an hour and I felt every eye on me. The organist played the theme song from *Gone with the Wind* and the fans cheered me like a welcome boy next door. *Lord,* I prayed silently, *just let me hit the ball somewhere.*

I wasn't looking at the fielders, the way I do now. I wasn't trying to decide whether I could drop a bunt in front of the third baseman or sneak one between the pitcher and the first baseman.

I wasn't looking to slap something through the left side of a pulled-in infield. I just wanted to do something other than embarrass myself. I swung with all my might at the first pitch I could reach, blasting a shot directly at Doug Flynn (who later became a friend and Christian brother) at second. I dropped that bat and flew out of the batter's box like my pants were on fire. All my pent-up emotion was channeled into that swing and race to first base. I was fast anyway, but with all the adrenaline pumping at that moment, I may have been the fastest runner in history. I knew it was a routine ground out, a hard two-hopper. I was so thrilled at just having made contact with the ball that I was flying down that base line. Out of the corner of my eye I saw the ball come up on Doug and hit him in the chest. The ball dropped to the ground, he grabbed it bare-handed, and fired to first. Safe! It was ruled an error, of course, but I didn't care. I was on base. As I look back on it, I'm surprised I was able to slow down before I hit the fence in right field!

Everything was new. I was on base as a big-leaguer, leading off, trying to interpret the sign from the third-base coach. I wasn't comfortable. I was overwhelmed. The bases were ninety feet apart, just as they had been since high school. The pitcher was sixty feet and six inches from the batter. The rules were the same. It's just that this was it, the top level. Every mistake would be magnified here. Every weakness would be taken advantage of.

At least my knees weren't shaking as badly as they had been in the batter's box. I wound up scoring a run and we won the game, but my big moment came in the seventh inning off Met relief pitcher Dan Boitano. I got around quick on an inside fastball and ripped it down the right field line for a double. Boy, that felt good. When the game was over I signed autographs for those fans who knew who I was and then got a little attention from the press in the locker room, because it had been my first game. Some of the Braves veterans were friendly and cordial, welcoming me. Most of them ignored me, which is the more traditional way to initiate a newcomer.

I was one of the last ones to leave, savoring every moment. Suddenly, it was all over. I wandered out of the locker room and through the corridors to the street. It was late. It was dark. The stadium was empty. The noise was gone.

I felt a deep hollowness in the pit of my stomach. After that incredible adrenaline rush, finally reaching my unreachable star, I came crashing back to reality. Was that it? Was that all there was? Had the journey been more important, more fun, more fulfilling, more challenging than the result?

Make no mistake, I was realistic. I realized I hadn't actually made it yet. There was no guarantee I would become a starter on the Braves or have a big-league baseball career, but I had poked my foot in the door. The future would be up to me and my performance. Yet I felt so empty.

Cabs slowed as they drove by, but I ignored them. The hotel wasn't that far away. All I could think of was how I had worked so hard and sacrificed so much for so long, devoting myself to baseball. All I had ever wanted was to make the big leagues. Now I had done it. I had reached the mountaintop, but I felt so alone and so empty. What made this so unfulfilling? I had overcome all the odds, rejected every negative argument from all those who said I was too small, too light, too this, too that. Back at the hotel I just sat on the bed. I bowed my head. *Lord, is this all there is to it?*

Was I down because there was no one to share this with? I called Eveline and just bawled.

"Why are you crying?"

"I don't know," I said. "I guess I just thought it would be so much more than this. I waited for this all my life, and now it's here, it's happened, and it's over. Just like that."

The next day three roses were delivered to my room. Eveline had sent one for my hit, one for my stolen base, and one for my run scored. She hadn't forgotten me. She was always there to support me.

The next game was easier. The novelty was gone. I still had to go to the bathroom when I heard the national anthem, and my hands were still cold until I got in the batter's box for the first time, but I quickly became comfortable with the stadium, the routine, the competition. I played forty games for the Braves at the end of that season.

I hated being alone. Coming back from road trips to an empty hotel room was not my idea of living. I called Eveline and told her, "I need you. I can't be here without you." Until the end of the season, we lived in a Marriott Hotel. That was the site of the first of only three major fights we've had in our lifetime together. Here's how Eveline remembers it:

"As much as I loved Brett, I was not going to be taken advantage of by a man again. Up until that time, he'd been perfect with me, so I was surprised when he didn't come back to the hotel one night when he said he would. Some old friends were in town and he and a teammate were going to go out with them and have some fun until about midnight. I was tired, so I went back to the hotel after the game and went to bed.

"At one o'clock he was still not back. Two o'clock and he's still not there. Now it's three o'clock, and I'm getting mad. I'm wondering, what does a guy do at three o'clock in the morning when he's out goofing around? I was already dreading that he was going to find some tall, beautiful thing now that he was a cool big-leaguer, so I had worked myself up into quite a state.

"At 3:30 in the morning I sat staring at the clock, fighting tears. And I made a decision. If he stayed out all night, if he did not come back by seven that morning, then when he got back I would be packed and gone. That would be the end of it.

"I was dozing fifteen minutes later when I heard his key in the lock. He tiptoed in and I faked a sleepy voice. 'What time is it, Brett?'

" 'Oh,' he whispered, 'it's about twelve o'clock.'

"I jumped out of that bed yelling. 'Twelve o'clock!? No, it's not! It's 3:45 in the morning! Three more hours and I would have been gone for good!' "

Eveline had a right to be mad, even though I had an explanation. I had had to find my own way back. The problem quickly became my lie about the time rather than the situation itself. She understood and forgave the details, especially when one of my teammates apologized to her the next day for keeping me out so late. I had never lied to her before, and I never have since.

"Brett's character has always been consistent since then," Eveline says, "and he's never tried to hide anything. He's never given me a reason to doubt what he says, so I don't. When he tells me something, I believe him."

At the end of the 1981 season, the Braves said they wanted me to play winter ball in Puerto Rico. Eveline thought she might like to go back and finish college, so I told her she had a decision to make. "Either you go back to school, or you go to Puerto Rico with me."

"That's an easy decision," she said. "I'm with you."

I went back to Libertyville for a week and she went home to Virginia. My parents tried to talk me out of taking her with me to Puerto Rico, but by then I was entrenched. I would not be apart from her. They weren't happy, but they knew I was twenty-four years old and could make my own decisions. I was wrong and they were right, of course, but that made no difference to me at the time.

Eveline and I met in Atlanta for the flight south. My plan was to get to Puerto Rico and then go over to St. Thomas, where we would get married. Eveline's mother pleaded with her on the phone, "You're my only little girl. We have to have a wedding here."

"Fine," Eveline said. "If you want a wedding, you plan it and tell us when it is, and we'll show up." She thought it would be nice to have a wedding, but it wasn't really necessary.

I had a romantic plan of how I wanted to make our engagement official. I was going to buy a diamond ring and place it on a rock underwater where Eveline and I would later go snorkeling. When we got down there, I would point to it and give it to her. However, my one credit card at that time had a limit of $400, and I wasn't able to buy the ring I wanted for her. All I could do was just tell her that story when I proposed.

Eveline accepted, of course, and she was impressed by my romantic intentions. "Just my luck," she said, "some fish would have probably come by and eaten that ring anyway."

We were both still just blithely moving along in our relationship, ignoring our parents, refusing to deal with what we were really doing. We were so in love with each other and really did love God that we convinced ourselves we were devoted to him, regardless of our behavior.

Puerto Rico was great and we loved it. There were several Christians on the team and we got involved in a couples' Bible study that we both enjoyed. We read, we studied, we prayed, we even told others about our faith. We didn't think we could be happier.

One night we were attending a Bible study run by pitcher Eric Show and his wife, CariMia. A bunch of other people were there, and we were having a great time. Eveline and I didn't realize we were deluded. We thought since we were fellowshipping with other believers and enjoying God together, we were okay. We both had a lot to say that night about the Scripture passage and about living by faith and loving God and all that. This was living! We couldn't imagine a better life.

We were soon to find out, however, that not everyone agreed our life was so perfect. Our wake-up call was just around the corner. We were without excuse and would not be able to defend ourselves.

REALITY
SETS IN

Eveline and I respected Eric and CariMia Show. We had learned a lot from them and always enjoyed their Bible studies. But after one meeting in Puerto Rico late in 1981, they confronted us. It had been a great meeting and, as usual, I was hanging around talking to everyone and would likely be the last one gone. As the couples chatted and drifted away, Eric and CariMia asked Eveline and me if they could talk to us. I said, "Sure, what's up?" Eric said, "You know we really care for you guys. We've been praying about this and feel led to say it. You're coming to these Bible studies and you're saying that you love the Lord and are committed Christians. We appreciate that you've prayed to receive Christ and that you seem to love God's Word, but frankly you're being hypocritical."

All of a sudden neither of us was animated. I was embarrassed. I knew where this was going.

Eric continued: "I mean, you say you love the Lord and you're committed to the Bible and what it says, but the fact is you guys are living together and you're not married. You're living in sin."

For once even I was speechless. What could I say? I glanced at Eveline and she looked self-conscious too. I would have loved to have been able to say that we knew exactly what he was talking about, that we had agonized over the same thing, and that we knew we needed to do something about it. The fact was, we hadn't discussed it at all. In the backs of both our minds, of course, we knew there was a proverbial elephant in the living room that was never mentioned. As Eveline says, "We just walked around it."

We had been doing what we wanted to do, regardless of what God says, and that's what sin is.

I cleared my throat and finally managed, "We really appreciate your being honest with us."

Eric pressed on. "You need to pray about this and decide what you're going to do."

Eveline and I nodded, unable to look at each other or at the Shows. We went back to our apartment in silence. Finally someone had made us face the issue, and we had to deal with it. "You know what?" I said. "They're right."

"I know," Eveline said. "Why are we doing this? This is wrong."

We agreed that Eveline should fly home right away, get her wedding dress, and help her mother plan the ceremony. We would not be together again until I got home from Puerto Rico and we were married February 13, 1982.

The day after the wedding we left for spring training in Florida. Eveline says we never had a real honeymoon but that life with me has been a honeymoon ever since. But the life of a big-league baseball player, especially in the early years, can be anything but glamorous.

Since the Braves began the season on the road, it fell to Eveline to drive from West Palm Beach up to Atlanta and get us settled in our apartment. We had arranged it, sight unseen, through some people who had once stayed there. Eveline followed a couple of other wives on the drive and then stayed with one of them overnight. The next day she set out for our apartment. Here's what she remembers:

"I was determined to have the place all set up by the time the Braves came back from their first road trip and Brett was ready to get settled in Atlanta. When I found the place we had rented, I gave the landlady our deposit and she gave me the keys and directed me to the apartment.

"As soon as I opened the door, I knew it was a disaster. I was already exhausted and stressed from the drive from Florida, and I was nervous about arranging for our first ever semi-permanent home together. I had done a lot of arranging of housing and leases, and I had a pretty good idea of what would make Brett happy. This definitely was not it. The flat was musty, dingy, and had lime green shag carpet. The walls in the bedroom, where children had apparently stayed, had been painted over stickers, which still showed through. An old brown refrigerator had a huge dent and a long scratch in it. I would die before I would ask Brett to stay there. It was awful.

"I just plopped myself down on the carpet in the empty living room and cried my eyes out. No, I decided, we're not going to stay here.

"I found the landlady. 'I'm sorry,' I said. 'I'm afraid we just can't stay here. Can I get my deposit back?' To my pleasant surprise, she was real nice about it.

"Now what was I going to do? I got in my car, still crying. I prayed, *Lord, I don't know where you want us. I don't know what kind of apartment you have for us. Just show me some place.* I'll never forget just driving and crying and praying, *Lord, please show me where to go.*

"I passed dozens of apartment complexes, trying to see the road through my tears. All of a sudden I came to one and just turned in and parked. I didn't know why. I went to the sales office and told them I was looking for an apartment. They showed me one, about the same price as the one I had just rejected, and it was perfect. I signed the lease, gave them a deposit, and moved in. I believe God directed me there, and not just because we thought we deserved a better apartment. I would find out late that summer exactly why God had that very apartment complex in mind for us.''

Despite having finished the year with them the season before, I had to prove myself to the Braves all over again in spring training. I made the team, and manager Joe Torre told me I would start the season in center field, leading off. My goal quickly became to keep that spot in the lineup and that position in the field for a nice, long career on that team. Was I ever naive.

The Braves, who had been awful in 1981, started the 1982 season on fire. We won and we kept on winning. Game after game after game. Two weeks into the season we still hadn't lost, and we were chasing the record for most consecutive victories to begin a season. I was leading off and playing center field, hitting in the .260s, walking, stealing bases, and believed I was with the best organization in baseball. On Wednesday, April 21, 1982, I went 2-for-5 and scored the winning run with a head-first slide in a come-from-behind victory to make us 13-0. The next day the *Chicago Tribune* ran a story by John Leptich entitled "Area Reject Helps Spark Streak."

The story told how, just six years earlier, I had been a defensive replacement at Libertyville High School, how five years earlier I couldn't make the varsity at Arizona State. "Today," Leptich wrote, "he's the lead-off hitter, center fielder, and a rookie catalyst for the Atlanta Braves."

The article quoted my old coach, Ernie Ritta, "I didn't see the major-league potential. He didn't do much as a junior, but he started to come on the last half of his senior year."

I told that reporter that Ernie Ritta had been the driving force in my career. I said, "He never really gave me a chance. He put me in for defensive purposes, I'd get three hits including a homer, and he'd still say I was a defensive player. I told him I could play, but he didn't believe me."

Surprisingly, the article quoted Arizona State Sun Devil varsity coach Jim Brock that he thought my "ceiling would be somewhere below the majors. He looked like just another good little player. He wasn't that good a hitter, but he ran extremely well. I just didn't think his running ability would carry him."

That was strange, because in an article earlier that year someone had asked Brock about me and he had said, "I never heard of Brett Butler."

It was nice that the article also quoted Bob Mavis, the Braves scout who signed me. He said, "I saw three things: He can run and he can hit, and the third thing is an intangible—he wants it bad. The major leagues was his goal. He said he was going to fight like the devil to make it, and he did. We're not capable of looking into their stomachs and their heads, but I believed him."

That was all right. I didn't mind Mavis taking credit for having discovered me, though he and I both knew Bob had signed me as a favor to Doc Parham.

Most gratifying was that the article quoted Bobby Cox, who had cut me last in spring training the year before and was now the Toronto manager. He said, "Butler played like heck in camp last spring, and when I saw him at Richmond during the strike, I liked him a lot. He would have been up at the end of the year anyway. He's a great lead-off man, something the Braves haven't had in years. He's got a real good chance to be Rookie of the Year in the National League."

Joe Torre said, "Brett reminds me of Lou Brock. He has the ability to get on base, and he has stolen-base speed. He can hit, and he can hawk the ball. The first day I saw him in camp, I liked him. He hustles. He's cocky, but he takes criticism. He's tough on himself, but he's not afraid to screw up. Maybe that's what got him where he is. Pressure doesn't bother him."

The article ended with a couple of quotes from me. They

make me smile now. They remind me of the guy I was then. I told Leptich, "The difference between the minors and the majors is coping with pressure. I think I can. I want to be like Pete Rose and Willie Mays. I want to hustle and give my all. Maybe I am cocky. I don't care what people think. I made the majors. If I believe in myself, I'm gonna be all right."

Well, that was a great, fun way to start what I hoped would be my first full major-league baseball season. But I had spoken too soon. I had made the majors in just barely more than two years, and while I showed a lot of signs of being ready, I simply didn't perform well enough to stay there. When the Braves finally came back down to earth and started losing, they had to start shaking things up to make the lineup work.

It was a bitter disappointment to be sent back down to the Class AAA Richmond club. I didn't even have time to get a uniform on, however, before the kid they had brought up to replace me got hurt. (Since then, the rules have changed and a player sent to the minors has to stay for a minimum number of days.) I was called back up, rode the bench for a few weeks, and was finally sent back down. I was upset and frustrated, of course, but Eveline was realistic. I was hitting just a little over .200 by then, and a promising young Terry Harper was hitting .360 in Class AAA. Eveline said, "You know what, Brett? Why don't you just look closely at the situation? If you were sitting in Richmond hitting .360 and Terry Harper was in the big leagues hitting .217, wouldn't you think they should call you up and send him down?"

I couldn't argue with that. She was sometimes hard on me. She would say, "Don't whine and complain about it. Just go down there and play as good as you can and work your way back."

She knew what worked with me. Sometimes she would challenge me and say, "We'll just see if you can make it back from there." That was the kind of motivation I needed. I knew what she was doing, but I let her do it anyway. She knew that to bully me and push me about my prospects would make me only work harder.

One positive thing about going back to Richmond was getting to play under Eddie Haas again. He was certainly no sentimentalist. When he saw me walking from the clubhouse to the field he hollered, "Butler! Get your butt over here! You're not in the big leagues anymore!"

There would be no star treatment just because I had had a few at bats in the big show. Everybody knew I was down there to work my way back, but he was going to treat me like anyone else. And I loved it.

I worked hard in Richmond, hitting over .360 in forty-one games. I wanted to be ready to come back whenever the Braves needed me, and for sure in August when the major-league roster was expanded from twenty-five to forty players for the last several weeks of the season.

Our landlords in Atlanta and Richmond allowed us to move back and forth as necessary during the season, which was a great help. I finally got called back up to the Braves in August, about a month before our first child was due. Eveline's mother came to Richmond in the middle of the month to help her pack for the move back to Atlanta. Eveline had planned to leave at ten o'clock in the morning, August 15. At nine o'clock her water broke.

I was with the Braves in San Diego. It was 6 A.M. there. I was asleep when Eveline called. She said, "Brett, my water broke and I'm going to the hospital to have the baby."

"What?" I'd heard something about water and something about a baby.

"I'm going to the hospital, Brett!"

"Uh-huh," I mumbled. And I hung up the phone.

A few seconds later the phone rang again. "Brett! Wake up! Brett! I'm going to have the baby!"

I flew back to Atlanta with the team that night and we arrived after midnight. I got word that Eveline had had a baby girl by

Caesarean section. The next day was an off day so I was going to catch an early morning flight to Richmond to see Eveline and Abbi. As we were getting off the team bus, Skip Carey, the Braves announcer (and son of Hall of Fame Cardinals, White Sox, and Cubs announcer Harry Carey) called me off to the side. He pulled a flight coupon from his pocket and handed it to me. "This is my gift to you and your wife," he said. I stared at it. It was good for a round-trip ticket anywhere in the United States anytime.

I was a rookie. I hardly knew him. But that gesture touched me. We still keep in touch occasionally. I'll never forget that gift. I booked a flight for early the next morning. When I woke up I called Eveline to tell her my plans. We talked about the baby and how exciting it was going to be for me to meet her, and suddenly Eveline said, "What time did you say your flight was?"

"At 8:45."

"Brett! It's eight o'clock now!"

"I can get there in a half hour," I said. I had forgotten that the airport was normally nearly an hour away. I raced out there, parked, ran in, and got to the gate just as the plane was taxiing away. It was the only time I ever missed a flight. I caught the next one to Richmond.

Hardly anything was open, so I stopped at an airport shop and bought some plastic roses in a white vase and a dress for a little girl. It looked tiny enough, but it was for a one-year-old. Abbi, arriving early, was even smaller than the normal newborn. Eveline got a big kick out of that. I was thrilled and she thought that was great. It was hard to believe I was a father, and I fell in love with Abbi the minute I saw her.

Everything was fine when I headed back to Atlanta for Tuesday's game, but that quickly changed.

Eveline recalls: "A whole bunch of problems hit after that. I developed a temperature, I had a sore near my incision, and they wouldn't let me see the baby. I was panicky. My mother tried to calm me down, but I decided to call Brett at the ballpark. I called

Fulton County Stadium and had them ring the clubhouse for me. It was the middle of a game. Someone said, 'We can't get him now. He's on the bench in the dugout.'

"I started screaming, 'He's not playing! He's sitting on the bench! You go get him and you get him now!' "

When I finally got to the phone, Eveline sounded so hysterical I was ready to hop a plane and go back to Richmond right then. But between me and her mother we were able to get her calmed. I assured her I knew she would be all right.

But she really wasn't. For several days she was not allowed to see Abbi because of her own temperature. She couldn't figure out why she had developed a huge hole beside her incision. She'd never had a baby before, so she thought maybe that was normal. Later one of the doctors told her that someone had dropped the knife on her stomach. It had a superheated blade that burns the flesh away, and it had caused this hole, which had produced a blood clot.

Then they left an IV in her arm for several days without changing it. The whole thing was a nightmare. It's amazing she ever had another child, but she says once she was able to hold Abbi and really bond with her, she forgot that ordeal.

While I traveled with the ball club, Eveline spent a couple of weeks at her mother's with the baby. Then she headed back to our apartment, the one God had led her to so many months before. She remembers what we both now see as one of those pivotal moments in our lives:

"There I was, getting to know my three-week-old daughter, and there was a knock at the apartment door. It was a girl about my age who said, 'Hi, I'm your neighbor from upstairs. I have a UPS package that was left for you at our place. And do you have a cup of sugar I can borrow?'

"I was struck by how quaint that sounded. A neighbor borrowing a cup of sugar. That's how I met Indy Cesari and eventually her husband, Steve. She's still my best friend today. Our kids have grown up together. Every time she got pregnant, I got pregnant. We have four kids each, three girls and a boy. I honestly believe God put us in those apartments so we could meet the Cesaris."

My future as a big leaguer was no longer a sure thing. I was just getting occasional opportunities to play and started very few games. The Braves, after that incredible 13-0 start, had struggled during the midseason, fell out of first place, and had to rally in the end to win the division and the right to face the St. Louis Cardinals in the play-offs. Though I hadn't had much to do with it, I was thrilled with the chance to be in the postseason in only my second year in the big leagues. I didn't know then how rare a privilege that would be.

I got some good advice during that time from a couple of Braves. I asked Jerry Royster if he thought I would ever make $400,000 a year like he did. He told me that if I stayed focused and stayed out of trouble and did my job, I would make a lot more than that by the time it was all over.

Al Hrabowski, a relief pitcher better known as the Mad Hungarian, also had good counsel for me. They called him the Mad Hungarian because of his ancestry and his act on the mound. When he was brought in he acted as if he were in a rage. He stomped around the mound. Between pitches he would turn his back to the hitter and step toward second base, talking to himself and slamming his fist into his glove. When he was sufficiently angry, he would return to the mound and throw as hard as he could. We all knew it was just an act. But with his dark eyebrows and bushy Fu Manchu mustache, he was intimidating to hitters. In private he was just a teddy bear.

He told me one day, "Brett, remember one thing if you remember nothing else I tell you. Don't take anything personally up here. To the owners it's just a business. Just realize they're going to use you and abuse you accordingly. It has nothing to do with you as a person. That's just the way it is. It'll be easier for you to deal with it if you know that in advance."

At the time I wasn't sure what he meant. I assumed that if I upheld my part of the bargain and did my job, the front office would take care of me. I couldn't argue with not getting much playing time that season, because I was barely hitting over .200. But surely, if I excelled, if I came back and showed them what I could do the next season, I had a future in Atlanta. I was convinced of that.

It must have taken too much out of the Braves to come back and win their division, because the Cardinals swept us in three games in the play-offs. I looked forward to the next spring. I had a new goal, a new challenge. I wanted to earn back a starting role and become a big leaguer who didn't get sent down to Class AAA every time he had a slump or whenever management wanted to shake things up. We had a winning ball club with a lot of potential, and there was also a lot of talent. That didn't bother me. Making it in the first place had not been easy. Staying would be no cakewalk either. That was just the kind of a challenge I needed.

AT LAST

I would play my first full season in the majors as an Atlanta Brave in 1983, but it sure didn't look that way in spring training or when the season opened. The year before, when I was not producing, I was told to use a bigger, heavier bat and learn to get the ball down in the infield, to try to get on that way. For a while I was actually using a 36-inch, 36-ounce bat, bigger than most of the power hitters. I thought that was overkill. I had already changed my game from the power hitter I had been in college to more of a slap hitter, a line-drive hitter, one who would bunt and get on base and steal a base and score a run. But I didn't need to use that huge tree trunk of a bat. Where had it gotten me the year before? I'd had 240 at bats and only 52 hits. A batting average of .217 wasn't going to keep me in the big leagues. I knew if I hit ten home runs and batted .250 for a season, I wouldn't be in the majors long. I knew what my role was. The gifts God gave me in baseball were first, speed, and second, my mind. I was able to understand how to get the most out of my ability.

Of all the managers I've played for, Joe Torre is one of those I respect the most in the way he handled things, but back then I honestly believed he would rather deal with veteran players than rookies. He was a veterans' manager. I had struggled at the plate, and before you know it, I was gone. Sent down. I had finished the season with the big-league club again, but come spring training it was clear I was not part of the starting lineup picture. It didn't even look as if I was in the works to make the opening day roster.

During spring training Joe called me into his office and told me he was experimenting with Bob Horner in left field. Dale Murphy was already established in center, and Claudell Washington was in right. He told me, "Brett, I know you worked hard and tried to get the job done, but I need to tell you, you're not in our plans at this level this year." In so many words, he was telling me I was headed back to the minors once we broke camp and the Braves headed north.

I said, "Joe, you know I did everything you wanted me to. If that's the way it's gonna be, I'm gonna go back to my small bat and I'm gonna play so good you'll have to keep me." I turned around and walked out of his office.

I thought it was a mistake putting Bob Horner in the outfield. He was an infielder. He had come up as a shortstop and then moved to third base. He was a great power hitter, but he was not an outfielder.

Eventually the coaching staff realized they were making a mistake, and within a week and a half, Bob Horner was back at third base. I was in left field. I would play in 151 games that year and hit .280. I had worked my way back to leading off and starting in the outfield, and I finally felt I had established myself as a big leaguer. At the very least, I felt I had established myself with the Braves.

They were an organization deep in talent, however, so I was always looking over my shoulder. I constantly wanted to keep my average up and my run production going so they wouldn't have a reason to send me back down.

During those early years in Atlanta and Richmond, Eveline's

and my relationship blossomed and strengthened. We made a pact never to go to sleep without saying we loved each other. We had our share of squabbles and arguments, and sometimes those "I love yous" were cordial or uninspired or even grudgingly spoken, but we never missed one. Another part of our pact is that we wouldn't be apart from each other for more than ten days. Sometimes that meant flying Eveline and however many kids we had at the time to some spot on a road trip where we would reconnect. Our goal was to put God first, husband-and-wife communications second, and kids third. Family has always been important.

We had also decided that while we might not always agree with each other, we would give each other the freedom to speak our minds. Often we agreed to disagree, and that was fine, but we were always able to sit down and talk things out.

I was the one who might get mad and yell and scream, but the bottom line was to clear the air. We both admit now that though we were deeply committed to each other, our commitment to God was still less than it should be.

We were active in Bible studies and baseball chapel, but it was simply because we knew that's what Christians should do. Our faith had not yet become a vibrant, living, personal thing, for the most part.

The second of only three major fights we've ever had happened during that 1983 season in Atlanta. Communication was never a problem with us, and in this case we probably communicated too well. It started innocently enough, as many wars do.

I loved to play golf, and Eveline loved to play and watch tennis. She had worked her tail off to find six great center court tickets for a big AT&T Challenge tennis match in Atlanta one night. We were going to meet Indy and Steve Cesari and another couple at a restaurant for dinner at 5:30, and then go to the tennis match.

That morning I had to play in a special charity golf outing where fans paid a certain amount for the right to play with the Brave of their choice. When my teammate, Bruce Benedict, came to pick me up, Eveline reminded me of our late afternoon and evening obligations. I said, "Sounds great. We're supposed to tee off at eleven, so figure three or four hours and I should be home in plenty of time."

When Bruce and I got to the golf course, it was packed. There were more people than the organizers ever dreamed there would be. They quickly tried to revamp the schedule. Now we were going to play in fivesomes instead of foursomes. Our eleven o'clock tee time came and went.

Now it's noon. Now 12:30. Finally we get started, and with several fivesomes ahead of us with players at varying levels of ability, it's slow going. When we make the turn after the ninth hole, there's no time for me to call Eveline to tell her I might be late. I could have easily had Bruce drop me off at the restaurant or even at the tennis match, if necessary, but I still thought we'd make it.

Eveline remembers that day all too well: "Meanwhile, I'm waiting at home. Three o'clock, four o'clock, five o'clock passes. No call from Brett. I'm getting madder by the minute. I called the restaurant where we were supposed to meet Steve and Indy and the other couple. I told them to go ahead and eat. Luckily they had the tennis tickets, so I told them to leave ours at will-call and we would see them later. Six o'clock passed. Then 6:30. Finally, at quarter to seven, the phone rings."

I should have been able to hear in Eveline's voice that she was upset, but like a dummy I just plunged ahead. I said, "Hey, Babe! What's up?"

She sounded like death. She said, "Where the h—are you?"

Now, that was a rarity. I said, "We got started late, and we just got done. I'm sorry I didn't call you, but just tell everybody we'll meet them at the tennis match."

Eveline said, "I just can't believe . . ." Click!

Now I was mad. She had hung up on me! I stood there in the clubhouse staring at the receiver, seething. A little old man sitting nearby studied me and said simply, "You shouldn't have called."

That cracked me up. When I quit laughing, I was still mad at Eveline. I called her back and said, "Fine, if you're so mad, I'm staying for steaks."

Eveline's reaction to that comment: "My brother Joe happened to be staying with us at the time, and he had to get out of my way. When I get mad, I start cleaning. I was flying all over that house, cleaning everything. I couldn't wait till Brett got home. I was going to give him both barrels."

Meanwhile, I was in the clubhouse banquet room with Bruce Benedict, waiting for our steaks. It didn't take me long to start feeling bad. I said, "Bruce, we gotta go." By the time he dropped me off at home, it was way too late to go to the tennis match. When I walked in, Eveline ignored me. I said, "Let's talk about this."

"I don't want to talk to you," she said. With that, her brother walked out the back door and waited in the yard. He didn't want to hear what was coming. Eveline said, "You're sleeping on the couch tonight."

That's when I lost it. "The h— I am!" I said. "This is my house, and there's no way I'm sleeping on the couch. I'll break down that door if I have to."

She gave as well as she got, telling me how inconsiderate and irresponsible I was and how mad she was. We both did a lot more yelling, but finally she calmed down and let me explain. I apologized for not having gotten back to her earlier, and she apologized for reacting so angrily. I can't say I'd want to go through that again, but making up almost made it worth it. Eventually her brother came back inside.

Our running joke, to this day, is that when I say goodbye to her on my way to play golf, I say, "See you tomorrow." She has decided not to plan anything, count on anything, or expect anything for the rest of that day or evening. That way, she says, she can't get mad.

* * *

On our road trip in Chicago that season to play the Cubs, I got a chance to visit my parents in Libertyville. During that time I ran into my old high school coach, Ernie Ritta. After the pleasantries were out of the way, he said, "Brett, what did I do wrong? What did I miss?"

"Ernie, you never gave me a chance to play. But I thank you."

He looked at me funny. "Why?"

I said, "Because even without intending to be, you were the driving force behind my success. I wanted to prove you wrong."

I have no animosity toward him. I still think he was one of the key elements in molding my determination to make it. I have to give him credit for that.

Something was happening to me that year that no longer happens to rookies. I was a brash, young, cocky kid, but I was often put in my place by the veterans. They would say, "Shut up, Butler. Don't speak until you're spoken to."

Many of the guys would tell me to go get them a cup of coffee. For others I had to take their bags up to their room. Once they even made me walk through a hotel lobby dressed like a woman, wearing high-heeled shoes, and serve a meal to Gene Garber and Gaylord Perry in their rooms. That was part of joining the fraternity. After I did those sort of humiliating things, I was one of the boys.

I knew it was all some kind of an initiation rite. I felt fortunate to be there and didn't mind embarrassing myself once in a while as a step toward acceptance. Sometimes the teams would have a kangaroo court and levy fines for silly things or give people embarrassing awards. At one such "ceremony," Dal Maxvill (our third-base coach) presented me with a stop sign. I had run through his stop signs on the base paths three or four times. I was always safe, but Joe Torre would get on me. "You'd better not be thrown out!"

"He doesn't know my speed, Skip," I'd say. If Dal had tried to hold me up and I ran into a tag, I would have been fined.

Despite that kind of rookie initiation, I don't remember ever paying for a meal that season. They knew I made a lot less money than they did and the veterans were happy to pick up the checks. The older guys would take me under their wings, walk me through stuff, and give me hints and advice. When I was a young player, those were the things that made a team close.

Frankly I think a lot of young ballplayers could benefit from the same treatment by veterans today, but they won't listen. They're millionaires before they ever come to the plate in the majors. They dress right out of *GQ*, carry briefcases, have entourages, and answer to no one. That doesn't describe everybody, of course. The good kids, the ones who listen, are the ones who last the longest.

On July 10, 1983, at Montreal, I had my first five-hit game. That year I would lead the majors with thirteen triples and set an Atlanta single-season record with thirty-nine stolen bases. As we closed in on the last few weeks of the season, the Braves were in the hunt for the pennant, and I was having the time of my life.

With about three weeks left in the season, the Braves traded the Cleveland Indians two players, plus a player to be named later, for Len Barker. Eveline and I sympathized with the two players who had to go to that godforsaken city, which hadn't seemed to see good baseball since the 1950s. Someone in the minors had once told us, "Whatever you do, don't ever let them trade you to Cleveland."

Eveline had told me, "I love you, and I'll go anywhere with you, except Cleveland."

Rumors began to circulate about who the "player to be named later" might be. I thought it would be Claudell Washington. Others speculated that it might be me. That was impossible. We loved Atlanta. We'd bought a home. Eveline was pregnant with our second child. I was starting, playing every day, having a great year. Why would they want to trade away their lead-off man?

One day Eveline's brother Joe called and said he had read in the paper that Ted Turner had let it slip. I was the player to be named later. I couldn't believe it and didn't believe it, but one thing I knew for sure: Ted Turner would tell me.

I know all the knocks on Ted Turner, but I always liked him. Some people thought he was too intrusive, spent too much time in the dugout and the locker room and micromanaging the ball club. Maybe he didn't know as much baseball as he thought, but at the very least, Ted was honest. For whatever weaknesses he may have had, a straight shooter is my kind of guy.

The next time Ted came through the locker room, I cornered him. "Ted," I said, "is it me? Am I going to be traded? You've got to tell me, for the sake of my family . . ."

Ted didn't say anything. He just looked at me, pursed his lips, and nodded. "Yeah," he said finally. "It's you, Brett."

I turned away shaking my head, stunned. We were right in the middle of a pennant race. Couldn't it at least wait until the end of the season?

The next day, baseball commissioner Bowie Kuhn announced that since it was already known that I was the remaining player to be traded, I had to go immediately to Cleveland and begin playing for the Indians. I guess he thought it would be unfair to both teams to have a player who was a lame duck, just like the commissioner. Still, I was convinced it wasn't fair.

I called my agent. "Can't something be done about this?"

"Like what?"

"I don't want to go. It can't be right that he's already announced it if I'm supposed to be named later."

"We'll have to see what the league decides," my agent said.

Frankly, that didn't sound like someone who was looking out for my interests. I had heard great things about an agent named Dick Moss, who seemed to know the ins and outs of all the legal hassles between the players' association and baseball ownership. I called him. "Isn't there some way something can be done? Why should I be the victim in this? I wasn't supposed to be named until after the season, so I don't think I should have to go until then."

"You don't," he agreed. "This was Ted Turner's mistake. If you pursue it, he'll probably get fined, but you'll be allowed to stay through the end of the season anyway."

"Let Ted Turner get fined!" I said. "He made the mistake, let him pay for it. I want to stay here for now."

Dick Moss went to work and did the job. He was right. The league changed its mind about making me go to Cleveland right away. I was allowed to finish out the season with the Braves, and Ted got fined $25,000. But he didn't hold it against me.

It was a little strange playing alongside the Indian I had been traded for, but it was fun to be in a big-league pennant race again. The wheels came off our championship wagon during the last day of the season. We lost to the Dodgers on that day, and they made the play-offs. Still, it was gratifying to see banners all over Fulton County Stadium, wishing me the best, opposing the trade, and saying such things as, "An Indian Is Still A Brave." Another said, "Butler, You Will Always Be In Our Hearts."

I hadn't reached the level I thought I was capable of as a big leaguer yet, but the Atlanta fans sure seemed to love me. We were going to miss them.

When it came time to negotiate my contract with the Cleveland Indians, I called my agent. "I know I said you could handle my contract again this year, but I really think I need to reward Dick Moss for what he did. You didn't seem to be able to do what I asked for and he did, so I'd like to make the move and have him represent me."

"Fine," my agent said. "If that's what you want to do, I understand."

After I had signed my contract, he called me back. He quoted a figure he said I owed him, based on reneging on my promise to have him handle my contract for the next year. I was silent. "If you don't pay me," he said, "I'll see you in court."

If he had just told me that he felt this was right and that he needed that income for his livelihood, I'm sure we could have settled on a reasonable figure. But because of the way he announced it to me, I decided I would not give him a dime voluntarily. I waited for the notification of a lawsuit, but it never came.

At the end of the season I got some good advice from one of our great veterans, Bob Watson. He was a pure hitter. He said, "Brett, when you get to the American League, bunt more. The pitchers usually have the advantage when you switch leagues, but they don't know you over there. Until they figure out that you can hurt them with a bunt, drop some down."

That would prove to be great advice. (That year I would hit only .269, but nobody complained because I had 42 bunt hits and became the first Indian in history to steal fifty or more bags and score a hundred runs in a season.)

I can't say I was excited about going to Cleveland, but during the off-season Eveline and I both came to the place where we accepted it. We were not going to sell our house and buy in Cleveland. I firmly believed I would just go there for a few years, do my best, and establish myself as a big-league player. Then I would move on to greener pastures, like most people did who played in Cleveland. The Indians were known as the farm system for the rest of baseball. Good players came through there, but they didn't stay.

I also believed the pressure would be off. In Atlanta, I always had to be careful not to go into a slump or let down for an instant. In Cleveland, I felt I would be able to relax. I mean, they had traded for me. I would be playing. They needed me and they didn't have a lot of young guys nosing around my position. That meant I would be able to do even better, I hoped.

Eveline, of course, had been kidding about not moving with me to Cleveland. Anyway, she recalled hearing Andre Thornton of the Indians speak at a Professional Athletes Outreach meeting, and she had read his book. She looked forward to the opportunity of meeting him in person. He was a wonderful, outspoken Christian whose wife and child had been killed in a car wreck, but somehow he had come through the tragedy, strengthened as a believer and still enthusiastic about his faith. Eveline and I knew we needed to get more serious about our faith. Perhaps Cleveland would be the place to do it.

I kept up with my parents by seeing them when we traveled to Chicago and by talking to them on the phone periodically. My father had never been a physically affectionate man, and he wasn't one for saying "I love you" either. We would have great talks on the phone, and he would always finish by saying, "Your mother and I are proud of you. Here's your mom."

One night in January I called to check on them and got to talking to Dad about how I still couldn't believe I had been traded "to Siberia. Spring training with the Indians will be a whole new experience."

"You know," he said, "Cleveland was my favorite team growing up. I never thought I'd live to see the day that you'd play in a Cleveland uniform."

That made me feel a little better. I had already thanked everybody in the Atlanta organization for letting me play for them. I remember believing that God had a reason for this and that I needed to trust him.

Dad and I talked a little more, but when we were finished, he didn't end with his usual sign-off. He said, "You know, son, I'm awfully proud of you, and I love you a great deal. Here's your mom."

Later that evening I commented to Eveline that my father had told me that he loved me. Not "your mother and I are proud of you," but "I'm proud of you and I love you." I also told her his comment about never thinking he would live to see the day that I would play in a Cleveland uniform.

GROWING

I idolized my father in the best sense of the word. I can't imagine having had a better dad. He was never harder on me than I deserved, and he was often easier on me than he should have been. In that way, he presented me an earthly picture of my Heavenly Father.

Dad wasn't perfect. He smoked too much, he worked too hard. He wasn't verbally or physically affectionate enough with us kids. But even those negative examples helped me. I never wanted to smoke, and, despite my upbringing, I've developed into quite a hugger. I hug my kids all the time, and even my friends are not immune.

My dad expressed his love in other ways. If I had a football game, a cross country meet, a basketball game, a wrestling meet, or a baseball game—if he was in town, he was there. He warmed me up, worked me out, and gave advice. He's the one who told me that if I could count my close friends on the fingers of one hand, I'd be a lucky man. Let me tell you something: I'm a lucky man.

As I sat thinking about how my father had closed our phone

conversation differently than ever before, I was reminded that once, while I was in college, I'd had a frighteningly realistic dream that Dad had died. Maybe you've had one of those where you don't know why or how or what happened, but you're at a funeral or a wake or people are just sitting around talking about the death of a loved one as if it was sad but true. It really shook me. I was twenty-one years old. The next time I was home on break I told Dad about it. I was worried about him. I knew he considered himself a Christian because we had been churchgoers all our lives, but ever since my experience at the Fellowship of Christian Athletes conference in Fort Collins, Colorado, in 1973, I knew that going to church didn't make you a Christian any more than being born in a garage made you a car.

My mother had been the one who opened the Bible to us kids and often read to us and told us stories and reminded us to do what Jesus would do. Dad supported all that but was less overt about it, and so I felt compelled to talk to him directly.

"Dad," I said, "I had a dream that you died. If you were to die tonight, would you go to heaven?"

"Yes, I would."

"Are you sure?"

"I know beyond a shadow of a doubt."

"How do you know, Dad?"

His answer thrilled me, because he quoted the very verse that convinced me of my own salvation.

"Because of Revelation 3:20," he said. " 'Behold, I stand at the door and knock. If anyone hears My voice and opens the door, I will come in to him and dine with him, and he with Me.' That's a promise, Brett. I opened the door of my heart to Jesus and he's promised to be with me to the end."

I don't remember Dad and me ever having so frank and specific a conversation about his standing with God after that. But I was sure glad I had asked him. I had not become an instant evangelist after I became a Christian as a sophomore in high school,

Baseball has always been my sport and my dream. Me in my Teamsters Local Little League uniform, my sister, Beverly, on her graduation from nursery school in 1967, and my younger brother, Ben, in his Dodgers peewee uniform.

My picture as a junior member of Libertyville Wildcats. I was too small as a 98-pound teenager to make the baseball team as a starter.

At the end of the baseball season in 1975, my senior year, I finally became a starter on the Libertyville High School team, hitting .400—but I had been to the plate only thirty-two times the whole season.

In first grade I wrote an autobiography titled, "I Want to Be a Major League Baseball Player." Yet I was always too small, the last one picked.

In June of 1977 I played in the NAIA World Series for Southeastern Oklahoma State University.

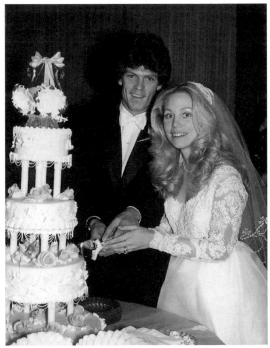

My coach at Southeastern Oklahoma State, Don "Doc" Parham, and I before a World Series game in San Francisco, October 1989.

My wife and best friend, Eveline's graduation picture from high school, 1978.

Eveline and I on our wedding day, February 13, 1982.

I was selected by the Atlanta Braves in the twenty-third round of the June 1979 Free Agent Draft.

My dad, Jerry, and I meet in San Francisco as he and Mom went to see their son play in the big leagues for the first time.

Pete Rose and I at Veterans Stadium in Philadelphia, September 1982. He signed a ball for me and said I was a "future .300 hitter." *Photo by Paul H. Roedig/Phillies photographer*

With Andi Newsome, a leukemia patient, in 1983.

Atlanta traded me to the Cleveland Indians on October 21, 1983.

Our family Christmas picture in 1986: Abbi, Stefanie, and Katie with Mom and Dad.

As my brother's best man at his wedding with Mom and my sister, Beverly, December 1988.

A Major League Baseball poster of me with the San Francisco Giants. I signed with them on December 1, 1987, as a free agent.

Running for first base in San Francisco.

Jan, Dave, Jan, Tiffany, and Jonathan Dravecky, Kathy and Scott Garrelts, and Eveline and I during the All-Star Break, Napa, California, 1988.

Eveline, Mom, and I following the earth-quake at the San Francisco World Series game, 1989.

On December 15, 1990, I signed with the Los Angeles Dodgers as a free agent. Here is the Butler family— Eveline, Abbi, Stefanie, Katie, and Blake—with Mary Morrisey, our nanny for eight years, at a Dodger Family Game in 1992.

Eveline, Stefanie, and I goof off at the Hollywood Stars game, 1993.

My best friend, Dave Hinman. We shared a dream of playing in the majors from the time we were blood brothers as children in Fremont, California.

Tommy Lasorda and I.

Our son, Blake, with Uncle Tommy during spring training in 1994, Vero Beach, Florida.

I split the season in 1995, playing for the New York Mets and the Los Angeles Dodgers and compiling a .300 batting average.

President George Bush and I during the play-offs in 1995.

Teammates and friends at our home in Atlanta: Todd Hollandsworth, Darren Hall, me, Dave Hansen, Billy Ashley, and Mike Busch (the controversial "replacement player").

Portraits of a leadoff man. My goal is to do whatever I can to get on base and get myself into scoring position. My career batting average, so far, is .291, but my on-base percentage is .378.
Photos by John Klein/Major League Baseball Photos

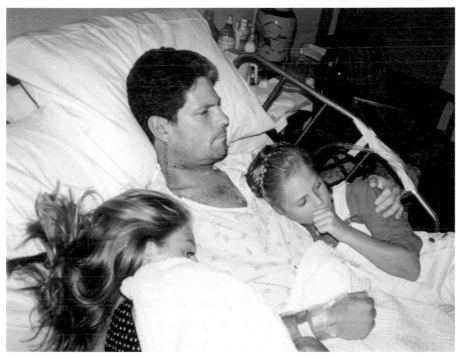

Abbi, me, and Katie at Emory University after cancer surgery, May 23, 1996.

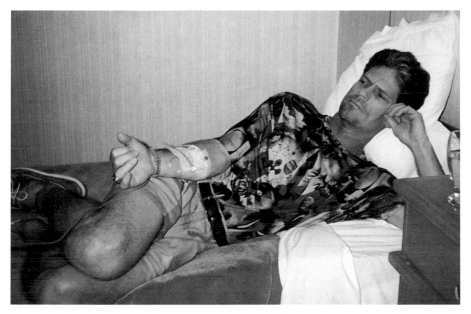

Receiving immune booster therapy at American Biologics in Mexico, July 30, 1996.

Me, Eveline, Abbi, Stefanie, Katie, and Blake at World Series Game 4, Atlanta Fulton County Stadium in 1996. Eveline wrote on the back of this picture: "Brett throws out first pitch!"

Eveline, Abbi, Stefanie, Katie, and Blake with me in New Orleans during my workouts for my comeback in August of 1996.

Steven and Indy Cesari, Eveline and I, Steve and Suzanne Dils, and Lowery and Vickie Robinson at Eveline's surprise birthday celebration, July 13, 1996.

My daughter Abbi, my little sister, Beverly, and I at the Olympics in 1996.

Eveline and I with my doctor, Dr. Bob Gadlage, and his wife, Kathy, when we appeared on *The Tonight Show with Jay Leno*, September 5, 1996, the night before my comeback.

Roy Firestone presents me with the Vince Lombardi Award, a symbol of courage award, in Washington, D.C., November 1996.

I thank the fans for their appreciation of my comeback on September 6, 1996.
Photo by Craig Jones, Allsport

but it wasn't unusual for me to ask people the same question that had brought me up short and caused me to make sure of my standing with God. I learned that a lot of people believe they are Christians because they have a head knowledge of God, but they don't have a heart knowledge. In other words, if you were starving and there was a plate of food in front of you, you'd still be starving unless you ate the food. At some point, you have to make a decision and take a step and eat the food. Or open the door to Christ, as the case may be.

Over the years I've been known as a Christian ballplayer, and at times people have accused me of being a little too enthusiastic or overt about it. Christian players often suffer from this criticism. People think we're trying to force our beliefs on other people. In my opinion, that can't be done. No one can be forced to become a Christian, any more than you can force a starving person to eat that plate of food. But what kind of a friend would you be if you didn't at least point out the meal?

I've never thrown the Bible at anybody. All I can do is present the truth when I feel the time is right. I do believe God has given me the gift of evangelism, because often when I share Christ with people, they're not offended. And many have received him. I try to wait for his leading. There may be a thousand people I'm speaking to and it might seem like a perfect time to share, but if God doesn't put it on my heart, I don't. Other times, I might be with just one or two people and it seems exactly the wrong time to bring up the subject. Yet if God seems to lead me that way, boom, I don't hold back. I feel obligated to let people know the good news of the truth that will set them free.

I've been called a hypocrite and I have been inconsistent at times. When I get criticized for that, I admit it and say, "I never said I was perfect. That's why I need Christ in my life." That usually opens an opportunity to share more.

The problem with most Christians is that we become judges, almost without realizing it. A friend of mine says, "We are not to be judges; we're to be fruit inspectors." If the fruit of your life shows you're not where you need to be, I'm gonna call you on it just the way I want you to call me on it.

It wasn't my place to call my dad on the carpet for anything lacking in his spiritual life, and except for the fact that he wasn't as vocal about his faith as I might have liked, there was little to criticize. I admired him and respected him and loved him. Besides being my dad, he was one of my best friends.

The day after that unusual phone call in January of 1984, my mother called. I could hear the panic in her voice. "Your dad just had a heart attack, and they've given him a 50/50 chance of making it."

I could hardly breathe. "I'll be there tomorrow, Mom. I'll call you back with my flight times."

Dad was a strong man, only forty-nine. I was sure he'd be all right. I told Eveline what was going on and called to make reservations. Then I called my mother back. Her voice sounded hollow when she answered.

"Mom?"

"He died!" she said.

I could hardly make it register. News like that has to be digested in small bites. "I'll be there tomorrow."

I hung up and sat on the floor. I just bawled. Eveline came and sat with me and cried with me. I was devastated. I couldn't believe it. He was still so young. If he had to go, why couldn't I have been there when he died?

On the plane I realized that one of my anchors in the world was gone. I was now the man of the family. I had always been protective of my younger brother and sister, but now I would also be responsible for my mother. I had always felt a sense of need to take care of my mom because my dad traveled so much. Now it would be a lifelong commitment.

When I got back to Libertyville, we all grieved together. I was curious, of course, about how it all happened.

My mother told me that my sister, Bev, and her fiancé, Paul, were over, and my brother, Ben, was home. That made me feel even more left out. How I wish I had been there! When our family is together, we always play something. A big card game in our family is Nerts. It's a take-off on Solitaire, a speed game. Mom said they were all sitting around talking and she said, "Hey, Jer, let's play some cards."

Dad said, "Ah, I'm just going to lie on the couch and rest a little bit. I don't feel good."

Mom and the rest of them had begun to play cards when she noticed Dad get up and walk into the bedroom. He didn't say anything, but he was always a private individual, even at home. Mom said, "Jerry, are you all right?"

He didn't respond. He just closed the door. She excused herself from the game and stepped into the bedroom, where she found him on the bed, lying on his back with his legs crossed. He had a hand over his face.

"Jerry! Are you all right!?"

"Betty," he said, "don't yell. I'll be all right."

But he didn't look all right, so Mom called the paramedics. At that time she was a clerk for the Village of Libertyville, so they knew her and knew exactly where she lived. They were there almost immediately. While the emergency medical technicians were trying to stabilize him, Mom thought of one of Dad's favorite phrases: "Us Butlers are tough."

Once Dad was settled into the hospital, she leaned over his bed and said, "Jerry Butler is tough. Hang in there." Within the next few moments, he was gone. Tough as he was, he couldn't survive the assault on his heart.

That next day was bittersweet for me. It was so hard to say goodbye to Dad, and yet I was warmed by the many, many people who came to his funeral. To me it was amazing, as if seeing my whole life reflected in those faces. I saw people I hadn't seen since peewee baseball, others from Little League, others from high school. Family, friends, neighbors, loved ones, they all filed through the family receiving line at the funeral home, each with something special and meaningful to say about Dad.

We flew his body out to Glendora, California, about half an hour from Los Angeles, where he was buried in the family plot.

I returned to Atlanta, still grieving, but also more grateful than ever for Eveline and Abbi and for the new baby that would soon arrive. Having to take responsibility for my mother and stay in touch with her more than ever would put a strain on our marriage, but I didn't see any way around that.

I don't want this to sound arrogant, but I never met anybody who had better parents than I did. To me, they were the best. That doesn't mean everything they did was right, but my parents were cool. Even my friends loved my parents. It was as if somehow my parents were different from everybody else's. (It's funny, because I hear a little of that about Eveline and me from Abbi now. She'll say, "Dad, my friends think you guys are so cool. But, of course, they don't have to live with you!")

The Cleveland Indians have been a great baseball team for the last several years, but let's be honest: Until recently, only natives of that area would have wanted to play on that team. Don't get me wrong, Cleveland is a wonderful city, and the fans are fantastic. Lord knows, they're long-suffering. No one knows why a team or a city goes through a period when they seem to be on the bottom rung of the big leagues, but Cleveland had more than its share in those years. And when I was traded there, they were in the depths of it. There were times when Eveline and I literally asked ourselves if God was punishing us or trying to tell us something by sending us there. One thing I knew for sure: if I couldn't play in Cleveland, I couldn't play anywhere. Going to a team with low expectations and not much talent in the farm system gave me an opportunity to establish myself. I had a feeling if I could have a great season or two there, I would be a top prospect for contending teams.

Sports Illustrated actually predicted that the Indians would win the World Series that year. I was pictured on the cover with three other Indians, and for a brief time it really did appear we had the nucleus of a great ball club. We had several .300 hitters, but we simply didn't have the pitching to back it up. I would play four seasons there, during which we would have two more girls, Stefanie and Katie, and my son, Blake, would be on the way soon. Needless to say, the kids were the highlight of the Cleveland experience. The Indians lost and lost and lost.

We never moved permanently from Atlanta, and we never will. It's home. My goal the whole time as an Indian was to play my way back to Atlanta. I didn't know how or if or when I would get there, but that was what I was after. I wanted to become such an attractive commodity to them, they would have to come looking for me when I was a free agent. It never happened, but it kept me going.

With all that said, you might get the impression that our four years in Cleveland were a total loss. Nothing could be farther from the truth. It was gratifying that on the baseball side, I hit almost .300 over those four years. In 1986 I led the majors and tied my career high with 14 triples, and was stunned to learn that I had become only the second player in major-league history to lead each league in triples.

But baseball is far from being my whole life now, and in Cleveland I learned to rearrange my priorities.

As I mentioned earlier, Eveline had heard about Andre Thornton's strong faith in the face of the tragic loss of his family, and she had wanted to meet him ever since. He was the slugging star first baseman of those Indian teams, and our meeting him and his new wife, Gail, proved to be all and more than Eveline expected.

Andre Thornton was a big, powerful man. An outstanding Christian, he commanded respect wherever he went. He was like God on our team. I can remember being in the clubhouse when guys were fooling around before the game. They'd be foul-mouthing and using the most vulgar language imaginable—which, sad to say, is all too common among big-league teams. Andre would walk in, and that would stop. He never had to say anything. He just had that kind of effect on people.

Eveline and I learned a lot more about Christ and the Bible than we ever had before while meeting with several Cleveland players and their wives. Andre and Gail were tremendous examples to us. Finally, we began to grow spiritually.

One day I was stunned to see a quote from Andre in the newspaper. He had been asked who he would want to be if he could be anybody in the world for one day. He said, "Brett Butler."

It certainly wasn't because I was a better person than Andre. He said it was because he was an introvert and I'm an extrovert. He apparently envied the way I could just gab all day long. I loved people and I loved getting to know them. I would ask questions about someone long after their attention span ran out.

I loved Andre so much, I just liked to hang around him. One time I was sitting behind him on the team flight and I was pouring myself a Coke when we hit an air pocket. The Coke sloshed into my lap. Always concerned about my clothes and my appearance, I quickly stood to try to brush it off before it soaked in and stained. Andre, totally out of character, turned and said, "If you can't drink it, wear it!"

I don't know what came over me, but I lost it. Here, was poor Andre trying to come out of his introverted nature and joke around a little with the boys. His comment was not unlike something anyone else would have said, but I was not in the mood for it. I laid into him. "I don't need that _____, you _____!"

Immediately, two young players in the back of the plane jumped up and slapped high-fives. One of them said, "Butler called Andy a _____!" There was laughing and cackling and high-fiving all around. I couldn't believe I had done it. Of all people for me to take out my anger on, it had to be Andre Thornton.

I said, "Andre, I'm so sorry. Forgive me."

The guys in the back were still carrying on, so I hollered out, "Guys, that's why I'm a Christian. I need Christ in my life to control my tongue and change me into the kind of person I need to be."

They would have none of it. "Aw, we don't want to hear that crap! We heard what you said! You claim to be religious, and you talk like that!"

I felt awful. Andre said, "Don't worry about it, Brett. Just forget it."

I didn't sleep well that night. All I could think of was the horrible name I called Andre Thornton, of all people. The next day at the park he approached me. He pulled me off to the side and said, "Brett, forgive me."

I said, "Forgive you? I'm the one—"

"No," he said. "If I hadn't provoked you, you wouldn't have said that."

Andre hadn't intended to, but if anything, he made me feel worse. That was the kind of character I wanted to have. I never heard Andre say anything bad about someone to anybody. He was one classy guy. I've had a lot of friends and met a lot of people in baseball, but he's probably the guy I respect the most.

What a lesson I learned from that whole situation! I needed to think before I spoke, to be humble (as Andre was) about provoking incidents, and to become a mature Christian like him. I wanted to grow enough in my faith to react the way Andre had.

Tom and Joann Petersburg, who work with Campus Crusade for Christ and handled the chapels for the couples, also had a huge influence on our spiritual lives. Finally, Eveline and I were doing more than just going through the motions. We were starting to become committed.

Joe Carter, who came from the Cubs to Cleveland, was another friend. I remember one year at the winter meetings between seasons, he was a free agent and could have gone almost anywhere he wanted. He had good offers from both San Diego and Kansas City, and his wife wanted him to go to Kansas City.

Joe, however, decided that San Diego was a great place, so he agreed to their deal. His wife was not happy, especially when San Diego traded him to Toronto the very next day. Now they had to go to Canada, and he was thinking, *You have got to be kidding me.* He called and said, "Brett, I need you."

I went down to his room and we knelt by his bed and prayed together and cried together. I told him, "Joe, there's a reason for this. You never know. You might go to Toronto and win a world championship."

He said, "Yeah, but my wife doesn't want to go up there. I should have done what she said. She wanted me to sign with Kansas City and I didn't, and now I'm traded to Toronto."

Baseball fans already know the end of this story. Joe Carter was on two world championship Blue Jays teams in 1992 and 1993. In the sixth game of the 1993 series against the Philadelphia Phillies (the Blue Jays were leading the series three games to two at the time), the Phillies scored five runs in the top of the seventh inning to take a 6-5 lead. In the bottom of the ninth, with one out and two runners on, Joe Carter won the game and the Series with onenb]of the most dramatic home runs in history—the only time a hitter has brought his team from behind to win a Series with a home run.

I understand both Joe and his wife, Diana, have fallen in love with Toronto, just as Toronto fans have fallen in love with them.

Eveline and I were finally getting into the Word every day on our own and often together, because of what we had been learning in the team Bible studies and chapels. I didn't know I needed one more wake-up call to set me on the right course spiritually, but it was right around the corner.

A NEW VISION

Eveline and I made a lot of friends in Cleveland who remain our friends today. I got close to my teammate Mike Hargrove, who's now managing the ball club. His sister was our nanny for a while.

One of the veterans I admired in Atlanta and became close to during the off-season (because he also settled in that area) was knuckle-baller Phil (Knucksie) Niekro. We enjoyed bowling against one another and would bet a quarter a game. He was pitching for the Yankees in 1985 when I faced him on August 8 in New York.

I worked Knucksie to a 3-1 count and then hit a home run on an inside fastball.

After another one or two hits off him, I hit another home run late in the game and the Yankees took him out. It would be the only time I would ever have two home runs in a game, but the Yankees came back and won the game.

When the game was over and I got to my locker, I found a baseball with an inscription on it. It read, "Brett, is there anything in this game you can't do? I wasn't surprised a bit. Knucksie." On the other side he had written, "Keep your quarters. I'll get you next time." That's how he was. All class. I'm so glad the Dodgers played in the Hall of Fame game on the weekend when he was inducted.

During one off-season in Atlanta while I was with the Indians, I left the house one morning to play racquetball. I had really gotten into the sport and enjoyed it. Eveline remembers that racquetball was a little like golf for me. I would play for only an hour or two, but I might be gone four or five hours.

She says that hours later, I might still be playing or I might be sitting around, because I'm a people person. I love to invest in people's lives. Most likely, I'd play for two hours and then sit at the club and talk to people even longer than that. I have to admit, she's right.

One day I was particularly late getting back from racquetball, and I finally called her.

Right away she was suspicious. "Where are you, Brett?"

"I'm at the hospital."

"Yeah, right. You're at the hospital. That's a good one."

"No, really," I said. "I took a racquetball in the eye and they're gonna patch my eyes. I'll have to stay here for a while."

Eveline still wouldn't believe me. "Oh, come on, Brett! You can come up with a better excuse for being late than that, can't you?"

I passed the phone to the nurse who was standing beside my bed. She said, "Mrs. Butler? This is Piedmont Hospital. Your husband really is here, and you might want to come down. This is a fairly serious injury."

Of course, Eveline felt terrible then and hurried to the hospital.

I remember very little about how the injury happened, except that I was wearing those kind of racquetball goggles that have no lenses but are designed to protect your eye by surrounding it with a thick frame. The ball is not supposed to be able to get through the small slit, but the one that rocketed off the wall and caught the frame around my right eye must have hit just perfectly, because it apparently had enough force to elongate itself and smack off my eyeball. It ruptured the cornea. I felt as if I'd been shot.

The doctors decided the only hope of regaining my sight was to immobilize that eye for several days. That meant both eyes had to be patched, because the right eye muscle follows the left. If I looked from right to left, that right eye would do the same. So both eyes were patched and I was given Valium to help me keep still for almost a week. I asked the doctor to estimate my chances of playing ball again.

"I don't know anything about that," he said. "I'd say there's about a seventy percent chance you'll regain vision in that eye."

I didn't like those odds. Odds had never bothered me before, but usually there was something I could do about them. How do you fight to regain your sight? It's a waiting game. It was out of my hands.

Eveline and I had become friends with Atlanta Falcons quarterback Steve Bartkowski and his wife, Sandy. They were Christians who had been very encouraging to us.

As I was lying in bed during those interminable days of fear and doubt and frustration at being unable to move, Steve called. He heard I had suffered an eye injury. "You know, Brett," he said, "as I was praying for you, I believe the Lord told me that your right eye will be better than it was before."

I always appreciated that Steve had a close walk with God, but I thought he was a little over-exuberant that day. For one thing, no one had told him my *right* eye had been injured. Also, he couldn't know this, but my vision prior to the injury was 20/20 in both eyes. I had astigmatisms, but that had not affected my perfect vision.

I should have realized that Steve knew what he was talking about (and that God did too, of course) simply because he had "known" without knowing that it was my right eye. Regardless, I was encouraged by his call.

I went through a depressing time lying flat on that bed all day. Eveline and I both realized that while we had grown and learned a lot, we still had a long way to go toward total commitment. Her life had been centered around the kids, naturally. At that time we had three daughters under the age of three, and even with help, that's a tremendous chore for a mom.

My life had revolved around baseball for more than twenty years. Now I was forced to consider the possibility that my career was over. If I had only a seventy percent chance of regaining vision, what kind of vision might I regain? Would it be good enough that glasses or contacts would make it perfect again? Would there be any possibility of my hitting without perfect vision or at least correctable vision? That was unlikely. For sure, I never would have been able to hit with vision in only one eye. Stereo-optical vision is required to judge the speed, movement, and location of a sphere you're trying to hit with a rounded object. The best hitters in the game have always had the best eyes, no exception.

Was I willing to give up the game? I didn't want to, but I had to face the fact that God might be trying to tell me something. It was not easy, but I had to come to that conclusion and be able to say to God, *Lord, if you don't want me to play baseball, if you want me to go sell cars or do something else, that's fine. I don't want to give up baseball, but I still want to be your bond servant. I believe you are the almighty healer, and if you want to, you can heal my eye.*

For six days I lay on my back, sitting up only to eat. Valium can relax you, but it's no way to live. The only thing I saw were imagined images. No light. No nothing. I was tempted to move around more, but I didn't dare. My eye had been ruptured by the racquetball, and it had to heal itself without interference.

I was scared to death the day the wrapping and the patches came off. This was done in a dark room, of course, and light was reintroduced gradually. I don't remember much pain, but it was scary to realize that my eye muscles had atrophied, my focus had to be relearned, and that my vision was so blurry at first. I was thrilled to know, however, that the vision in both eyes seemed equal. My left eye, the healthy one, needed to be retrained, and I needed exercise to build it up. The right eye seemed to be in the same state, despite the injury. Was it possible it would heal completely?

Over the next several days, my vision cleared. The exercises rebuilt the muscles, and soon it seemed I could see as clearly as ever. Just before it was time to go to spring training for the next season, I had a thorough exam. My left eye was still 20/20, of course. My right eye tested, just as the Lord seemed to have told Steve Bartkowski, at 20/15—better than before. That racquetball had leveled out the astigmatism, and I actually had better than normal vision. Interestingly, I've been a slightly better hitter ever since. Some of that has come with maturity and experience, of course, but there's no substitute for a gift from God—great vision.

Eveline and I truly believe we became different Christians from that point on. Her life still revolves around me and the children, but we are not first place with her and we know it. Christ is her Master. She has her own devotional life aside from church and chapels and Bible studies and devotions with me. I'm the same. We realized that our priorities had been out of whack and that we needed to get back to our first love, Christ. A lot of people who call themselves Christians just float along, letting all their spiritual input come on Sundays, if they're listening at all. We have found that the most vibrant and real believers are those who put their relationship with Christ first and spend time every day reading the Bible, praying, and building each other up in the faith. We learned this the hard way by making a lot of bad decisions.

In no way am I saying that we're perfect or that we're better than anyone else. We still fail. We're still inconsistent. There's still that temptation to skip Bible reading and prayer. When those slumps hit us, we're more out of sorts than ever. But that frightening, almost career-ending injury really caused us to adjust our courses. For that reason, scary as it was, I wouldn't trade the experience for anything.

My old friend Bobby Harju remembers that he noticed a difference in me around that time too. He was living in Zion, Illinois, with his family. One weekend the Indians were in Milwaukee to play a short series with the Brewers, and Bobby invited me to come down to Zion after Saturday's game and stay overnight with him. He and his wife, Skeeter, would drive me back the next morning for the Sunday afternoon game.

My mother, my sister, Bev, and the Harjus were all at the Saturday night game. Cleveland manager Pat Corrales took me out in the seventh inning, so I decided to shower, change clothes, and sneak up into the stands to surprise my family and friends.

"We're just sitting there watching the game," Bobby recalls, "a little disappointed that Brett is no longer playing, and all of a sudden, somebody plops down in the seat next to me. It was Brett in his street clothes! I said, 'What are you doing?'

" 'Quiet! I'll get in trouble if Pat sees me.'

"Brett was having a great time, hollering at the umpire, calling the vendors over, and we were all laughing our heads off. With just enough time to get back to the clubhouse before the game ended, he left. What a character!"

That night I rode to Zion with Bobby and Skeeter and we sat up till the wee hours talking. I hadn't seen him for a long time. At about two o'clock in the morning, Bobby started acting like we should get to bed because I had a big game tomorrow. I said, "What's the matter, Bobby? You tired?"

"Yeah, I'm kind of tired. But I'm just thinking of you, Brett. We've got to get you up and fed and off to Milwaukee in time for that game tomorrow."

Bobby remembers: "Brett seemed to care a lot more about me and catching up on old times than he did about baseball. I kept saying we ought to get to bed, and he kept saying, 'C'mon, Bobby, stay up with me and talk. It's been a long time.'

"That was Brett. Friends mean more than baseball to him. He said he could sleep on the plane after the Sunday game, and I shouldn't worry about him. We got only about three hours sleep that night, but we made the game in time and he had a good one."

It's sad when God has to use something bad to bring about something good, but often that's the way things happen. Eveline and I cared very much about our friends, Steve and Indy Cesari. They were dear people, loving and kind and friendly and helpful, but we were fairly certain that neither of them had really trusted Christ. Steve was a New Yorker with a rough background and was sometimes cynical and distrustful of others. We prayed for them a lot and looked for opportunities to share our faith with them. For some reason, as close as we were, those times didn't come for several years. It simply never seemed appropriate or right until it was God's timing.

God's timing with Indy came in the late 1980s when she and Steve left the country for a vacation. They were called home when her daughter Stefany, then a toddler, badly burned her feet in a bathtub accident.

There can be no worse pain for a parent than seeing a small child suffer. As that baby endured skin grafts and the trauma of all that hospital attention while going through such pain, Indy came to the end of herself. She knelt by her baby's hospital bed and prayed, *Lord, I can't do this on my own. I need you.* And she didn't mean she needed God only to get her through that ordeal. She received him into her life. While it would be a few years before Steve would understand what happened to her and she would feel free to get active in church and really start to grow, she was born again that day and became a new person.

Fast forward to 1990. Steve and Indy, our dear friends, are in

Atlanta. We're sitting in their kitchen, having enjoyed dinner and lots of conversation. By now I'm with the San Francisco Giants and have a multi-year contract. Eveline and I had been talking quite a bit that evening with Steve and Indy about feeling so blessed and so fortunate at how the Lord had watched over us.

Usually I'm fairly sensitive to how people are reacting. We were not witnessing to them necessarily, but I felt we were sort of doing a commercial for the goodness of God. Somehow I missed that this was rubbing Steve the wrong way.

Steve was and is a good guy, a hard-working entrepreneur. At that time he had a full-time job and was also trying a few projects on the side, trying to get ahead. Things weren't working out, and perhaps he resented that I was doing so well. For whatever reason, at about eleven o'clock we were virtually on our way out the door when Steve apparently could hold his true thoughts no longer.

Steve had always been one to speak his mind. He didn't hold back. That was something I liked about him. Still, as well as I knew Steve, I wasn't prepared for his comment. I had just said, "Hey, thanks for everything. We gotta go."

Steve said, "You know, Brett, I look at you and all I see is a hypocrite."

I flinched and shot him a double take. Then I looked at Eveline, who was also stunned. Indy looked embarrassed.

"What? Why?"

"You sit here and talk about how you know the Lord and God's first in your life and all this stuff, but I see you on TV and at the games. Just like anybody else, you get mad and throw your helmet and throw your bat. I've even seen you yell at your kids."

I sat back down. "Steve," I said, "we've got to talk about this. I never said I was perfect. I'm just forgiven. I'm just like anybody else. A sinner. All we're saying is that we're saved by grace, not that we're better or perfect or above anybody."

Soon we were all seated again. Steve said, "Well, look at you two. Everything comes easy to you. Everything has been handed to you. You've got looks. You've got talent. Why shouldn't you be Christians? It's easy when you make three million a year. You have everything you want and need."

We knew Steve's background. His father had died when Steve was fourteen. He'd been raised by his mother and had seven brothers and sisters. When he was sixteen, his four-year-old brother drowned. He also had a twenty-year-old brother who died in a car accident two weeks before graduating from West Point. Steve's legs had been badly burned in a fire when he was a child. His question, just as Eveline's had been, was, "If God was such a loving God, why would all these terrible things happen to me?"

I didn't have the answers Steve was looking for that night, and I still don't. Some things are impossible for us to answer on a human scale. But I knew someone who did have the answer, and she was sitting right there next to me. I turned to Eveline. She raised her eyebrows, knowing what I was thinking. I nodded. "Babe, I think it's time you told him your story."

I prayed silently as Eveline spoke. "Steve," she said, "I know exactly where you are, because I've been there."

Neither of us remember how long it took for her to recount virtually her entire life story, the sad childhood, all the tragedy that followed her up through college, the neglect, the abuse, the anorexia. She held nothing back. We loved these dear friends and there was no point in keeping any secrets now.

By the time Eveline finished her story, the four of us were sitting on the floor of their kitchen. Tears were streaming down Steve's face. Hours after we should have left, Eveline was telling Steve that he needed what she had needed—to receive Christ into his life.

That's just what Steve did that night. What an incredible turn-around there has been in his life since then.

We all hugged and cried and prayed some more, and then I told Steve, "There's something more you should know. Satan does not like it when someone comes to the Lord. There will be things happening in your life that will make you wonder what you have done. You're going to see things happen that will make you wonder what's going on. But we'll pray for you, and you stay close to the Lord and know that no matter what comes, he'll get you through it. Hard times will come. It's not *if* we struggle, it's *when* we struggle.''

Eveline and I were thrilled for Steve, and for Indy, whose husband now shared her faith. But we also worried about what was to come. None of us had long to wait. The next night Steve called. He had been fired from his job.

That was just the beginning of the trials he would go through after turning his life over to Christ, but he and Indy have survived and prospered. They remain two of our closest friends in the world. We consider it the highest privilege to have been able to play a small part in Steve's coming to Christ, even my humanness and inconsistency was the catalyst.

Though I may have gone to Cleveland kicking and screaming, after three seasons there, I actually wanted to stay. We had met many wonderful friends and had some great experiences, though the team had never turned around. We probably would not have moved from Atlanta permanently anyway (we rented a home in Cleveland during the season), but I felt I had earned a long-term contract. My performance and statistics put me at a place where I should have been able to get a very good three- or four-year deal at a salary commensurate with a starting outfielder who was able to produce runs. My agent, Dick Moss, agreed.

We went in to Peter Bavasi's office to see if Cleveland would extend my contract and were stunned when the Cleveland brass told me they didn't offer long-term contracts to players with less than six years of service. I had only five. I said, "How many guys want to stay in Cleveland? I want to stay and help this club."

Peter said, in essence, "Brett, the era of baseball is going to change. There's not going to be as much player movement as there was before."

When we left there, having been told they would not offer a long-term deal to just a five-year player, Dick said, "I want you to remember what you just heard." I remembered it. I remembered it until the day the owners were charged with collusion and had to name all the free agents during that period what was termed "new-look free agents." A number of us were free to start over and negotiate without fear of being shut out by the owners.

Maybe Cleveland already saw me as too outspoken. I wasn't afraid to speak my mind. It wouldn't be long before my mouth would get me into trouble with the brass.

ALL
SHOOK UP

My teammate Joe Carter led the American League in 1986 in runs batted in and was generally considered among the top five players in baseball. Yet the Indians offered him a *cut* in salary for the next year. I was incensed. Joe was insulted and walked out of spring training camp in 1987.

In my mind, the only two other players in Joe Carter's category that year were Eric Davis and Kirby Puckett. Those guys were both making about twice what Joe was offered. When he left camp, the press came to me. They knew I'd be good for a quote or two. They were right.

"I think it's disgusting when a man leads the league in RBIs and his front office says there isn't enough money to pay him what he's worth," I said. "They're implying that no one else would pay him more than he made last year either. He should be rewarded for the kind of year he had. I can't see how the Cleveland brass can look themselves in the mirror and believe what they did was right."

When the press moved away from me, I saw Andre Thornton on the bench, looking at me with his head cocked. His look meant something. "What?" I said.

"Did you say everything you wanted to say?" he asked.

"Yeah, why?"

"You'll learn from this, Brett. It wasn't your fight."

The next day I was on the field when I was called into the front office. I couldn't wait to get there. Joe was my buddy. I was hurting for him. I was going to fight for him.

The general manager was fuming. He told me, "I've never been so humiliated in my life. If I was a younger man, I'd kick your butt."

"Well, you're not," I said. "Answer me one question, just one: Are you telling me there's no market out there for Joe Carter to make more than you've offered him?"

"No, there isn't."

"You're lying to me," I said. "You know what the Twins gave Puckett and what the Reds gave Davis. The market is there! The thing I don't understand is that if you had offered Joe even a small increase with some sort of a graduated deal, he'd want to play here. But now, because you've ticked him off, he's going to take you to arbitration every year until he's a free agent and then he's gonna be out of here. Is that what you want for this organization?"

"I've got nothing more to say you to, Butler. Get out of my office."

The next day I found out he wanted to trade me to Oakland for a utility infielder, but he never got the approval. I didn't want to step on anybody's toes, but I saw someone who'd been hurt, and I had to come to his defense. That's always gotten me in trouble. I had to admit, in the end, that Andre was right. It wasn't my fight, and getting in the middle of it probably cost me my future in Cleveland. Andre taught me a lesson.

* * *

One night late during my years in Cleveland, I was awakened about three o'clock in the morning when Eveline sat up in bed, trembling. "What's wrong?" I asked.

"I just had the most bizarre dream, Brett. We were playing in the World Series. It was the Indians against the Braves, but for some reason we were in San Francisco. There was an earthquake, and the world ended. People were trying to get out of the stadium. It had collapsed. All I remember is that I couldn't find you and I couldn't find the kids. I was there by myself and I had my Bible in my hand. It was so weird. As we got out of the rubble, I looked up and noticed a hill, and then I woke up. It scared me."

I held her and didn't want to make fun of her dream, but I said, "Well, I don't see the Indians ever making the World Series, but if it's against the Braves it won't be in San Francisco."

"Brett," she added, "I was in a black Volvo on the way to the stadium with three women."

"Who were they?"

"I don't know."

It shouldn't have surprised me at the end of the season when I got a lukewarm reception from the Cleveland brass when I wanted to re-sign for 1988. Besides the fact that the owners would eventually be exposed for their collusion in not paying big dollars for free agents anymore, I had become too outspoken for Cleveland's taste. I was young and brash and opinionated.

Collusion had been the only explanation for why the market had dried up for free agents, especially those who had been producing. It seemed every team Dick and I talked to trumped up some reason for not being interested in me. Al Rosen, general manager of the Giants, was the only one who showed any interest at all.

I had always wanted to play in Los Angeles, which I saw as the classiest organization in baseball. I had been born not far from Chavez Ravine, before the Dodgers moved out there, but I had been raised in the Bay Area, so playing for San Francisco would be neat too. We were offered a three-year deal for four million dollars, which was a lot of money at that time. The market had not really ballooned the way it has now, but I was glad to finally get out of Cleveland and be on my way to San Francisco. They already had a good ball club, and I thought we had a chance of winning. That was the bottom line with me.

I was elated with the money too. When Rickey Henderson signed for around twelve million dollars for three years, people encouraged me to go back and renegotiate. I said, "No. My father taught me that once you put your name on the line, it means you're content with something and you leave it there." Two-and-a-half years later I would be awarded the status of a new-look free agent, and then I would go back and renegotiate.

My son, Blake, had been born in October of 1987, so we now had four children, ages five and under. It was good to know I would be able to provide for them and that I had job security for at least a few years.

When Eveline and I went to Candlestick Park in San Francisco to sign the contract for the Giants, she began shaking as we came out of the offices and headed back to the car. "What's wrong?" I said.

"Brett, look. There's the hill that was in my dream."

"C'mon, Eveline . . ."

"This is really strange."

I didn't put much stock in stuff like that. I urged her not to worry about that dream.

The Giants held their spring training in Scottsdale, Arizona, and it was there one of the great legends of the game urged me to come with him to visit children in the hospital. I learned a lot from that. But a few days later that same legend came into the locker room before a game and shouted in front of everybody,

"Butler, come here! I just got a phone number for you from a girl in the stands who wants you bad."

I just smiled and shook my head.

"C'mon, man. I mean she wants you, and she's something!"

"Not me, I'm a family man."

"So am I, but that doesn't mean I'm dead. You should see this woman!"

"Sorry," I said. "I'm a Christian. Can't do that."

"I believe in God too, but even he would want you to have a woman like this!"

By now everybody was watching and listening. Unfortunately, I had to go on the offensive. "You know, maybe it's time you got your priorities in order."

I had spurned him, shown him up in front of people. He turned and walked out. Even the biggest of the big have feet of clay. I had learned the hard way that life is about doing what is right rather than what is easy. It was hard to stand up to someone I admired that much, but it was important from my point of view.

There were more Christians on that San Francisco ball club than on any other team I've ever played on. A quartet of pitchers—Dave Dravecky, Scott Garrelts, Jeff Brantley, and Atlee Hammaker—lived in the same area I did. By 1989, pitcher Bob Knepper would join us. We became known as the God Squad, but it was not usually a complimentary term. Some thought we came on too strong. Some thought we would be weaker ballplayers because we were "too religious." We all fought that charge. I think all of us would have played the game as hard as possible within the rules, whether we were Christians or not. And those Christian pitchers weren't afraid to pitch inside either.

Anytime the Giants had a losing streak, there were those who wanted to get rid of the God Squad. Some even thought that's what Al Rosen eventually did.

When I first made the big leagues in Atlanta, veteran Claudell Washington told me, "You've got to make your own niche. You've got to do something a little different than everybody else." I remembered that advice and now, with a little more money in my pocket, I started dressing nicer. I bought a bunch of double-breasted suits and nice accessories. I also liked to wear fedoras.

When I got on the bus one day in Chicago wearing a fedora for the first time, Mike Krukow said, "Hey, check it out! It's Bugsy Malone. Give him a tommy gun and he'll be ready to go."

The name Bugsy, fitting so nicely with Butler, stuck.

I fell in love with the city of San Francisco, and I still believe the 1989 Giants were the best team I have played for. We had quite a run in 1988, though we would eventually lose out to the Dodgers and be overshadowed by Orel Hershiser's amazing year.

One of the highlights of 1988 for me was playing under manager Roger Craig. He was an all-right guy and not a bad manager, though he always told us to get him into the seventh inning and he would win the game for us. No one quite knew what to make of that. We didn't think he was such a great strategist that he could actually win the game from the bench. We still had to perform.

Roger had been a pitcher in his day and had lost more games than he won, though it's only fair to add that he was stuck for a few years playing with the hapless Mets, who set records for losses. Roger set a big-league record with more than twenty consecutive pitching losses in 1962, but on the other hand he had ten victories for a team that won only forty the entire season. That meant that while he was setting a record for futility, he was also winning twenty-five percent of his team's victories.

Roger Craig had a trademark: He hollered "Hum baby!" all the time.

Rick (Big Daddy) Reuschel was finishing a long career as a good producer for the Cubs and the Yankees, and he didn't like Roger Craig trying to tell him how to pitch. Late in the season during a tight game, Roger called time out and walked to the mound. Big Daddy gave him a look and said, "What are you doing out here? What can you tell me about pitching? Get your tail back in the dugout and don't ever walk out here again!"

By the time Craig was just across the third-base line heading back toward the dugout, Big Daddy was in his wind-up. When we came in between innings, Roger told Reuschel, "Don't ever show me up again."

Big Daddy said, "Then don't ever come back out on the mound. I know what I'm doing. I don't need you to come out and tell me how to pitch."

To Roger's credit, he didn't hold a grudge against Rick for showing him up. Later a flashy rookie was complaining that he was out in the sun running his sprints while Big Daddy was sitting on an exercise bike in the clubhouse reading a book.

Roger told him, "Son, when you've been in the big leagues long enough to earn that kind of respect, you can do whatever you want."

"Yeah, but he's out of shape," the rookie said.

"You think so? I'll bet you even money he could beat you in a race."

"There's no way."

They raced. Big Daddy beat him. That was the end of the criticism.

I've always been a statistics junkie, and for some reason I had seen Roger's numbers on the back of a baseball card. One day he was lecturing the pitching staff at a meeting, and he said, "Hey, if you guys don't get your act together, I'm gonna have to come out of retirement."

"Who are you kidding?" I hollered. "You lost over twenty games in a row in 1962."

That brought laughter, but Roger got his dander up. "Yeah," he said, "but we only won forty that year, and ten of those were mine!"

He rattled off a bunch of other statistics to show the type of a pitcher he really was, and when he finished I just smiled at him and said, "Hum baby, Rog!" Everybody roared, including Roger.

We had a powerful offensive arsenal and a bunch of scrappy players on our 1989 Giants. I turned thirty-two in June, and it seemed like the next day I started feeling all my aches and pains as never before. It used to be I could stretch a hamstring or twist an ankle or even bang into the wall, and by the next day I was fine. Now I would wake up sore and have to remember what I had done to cause it.

When I started to complain about it, Eveline squealed, "I have to call Andre!"

I knew what she meant. Andre Thornton was our grand old man when I was with the Indians. He seemed to spend more time in the whirlpool than anywhere else. Our nickname for him was "Thunder," and someone christened the whirlpool the "U.S.S. Thunder."

That's all I needed, Andre Thornton finding out I was becoming an old man too. He had predicted it. "You'll spend a lot of time in here yourself some day, Butler."

I knew the 1989 Giants were going somewhere. We had a catcher, Bob Brenly, who really knew how to call a game. And he was the type who would tell somebody who got spiked, "Chew some tobacco, spit on the wound, and let's go get 'em."

At first base we had Will Clark. To me he was like The Natural, a young phenom with an unorthodox swing nobody else could match. He had a little chunky body and short arms and legs, but he could generate tremendous power. At second base we had Robby Thompson, who was willing to get in the dirt. We called him Pigpen. He was the kind of a guy you could shoot from the stands and he'd still go get the ball.

Our shortstop was Jose Uribe, a rambunctious player with a great smile. He lost his wife in childbirth early that year, something that brought all of us together. The families pitched in and cooked him meals and tried to encourage him. You never know what's going to bring a team together, but camaraderie is crucial for making a run at the pennant.

Matt Williams played a lot of third base for us, as did Chris Speier. Matt was a struggling young player destined to become a star. Speier was a veteran who brought maturity to the infield.

The outfield was made up of Kevin Mitchell, Candy Maldonado, and me.

Kevin was the best player on our team and the MVP of the league that year. But there were times when he simply didn't want to play. On several occasions, one of our coaches, Bobby Bonds, had to ask his old friend and teammate Willie Mays to come and talk Kevin into playing. But once he played, wow, he was awesome. If it wasn't for Kevin, we wouldn't have won the pennant and made it into the World Series against the Athletics.

Most of our pitching staff that year was like the walking wounded, a MASH unit. But we had tremendous offensive power. We could be down six, seven, eight to nothing, and we still believed we would win.

One of the single greatest highlights of my life and career was playing center field in September 1989 when Dave Dravecky came back from cancer to pitch again in the big leagues. He was part of that God Squad, and all of our families were close-knit. We prayed for each other, we studied the Bible together. I remember the first time Dave complained about a lump in his arm and we all tried to speculate what kind of scar tissue it might be. When they removed the cancer, they took part of his deltoid. He told me, "The doctors say I'll never pitch again, but if God wants me to, I will."

I said, "I know, Dave. I believe that."

He was very strong in his faith, and his wife, Jan, and Eveline had become good friends.

The doctors didn't believe Dave would ever regain enough strength to take the wallet out of his pocket. They definitely didn't think he'd pitch again. He told them, "It has nothing to do with what you say. If God wants me to pitch again, I will."

Dave prayed that God would let him go out on the mound just one more time. We were all praying the same thing. When he miraculously got his strength back, he pitched a couple of games in the minors to get himself tuned up. Then he was ready to pitch for the Giants again. We were in the middle of a stretch drive, and Candlestick Park was packed to the gills.

There was World Series excitement. We were playing an important game against the Cincinnati Reds. Mackie Shilstone, a sports performance expert who has worked nutritional and conditioning miracles with lots of players (me included), was there with Dave and Atlee and Scott and Bob Knepper and me. Before we took the field, we went into a back room by ourselves and prayed. We wanted God to be glorified through the whole thing, from the way Dave carried himself to the way he performed.

I went out to loosen up while Dave was still on the training table getting a rubdown. As we were running our sprints, he came out of the clubhouse and walked onto the field to start throwing. An array of reporters and photographers had taken positions down the base line. As Dave walked through that group of flashing cameras, the fans went nuts. "Welcome Dave" lit up the scoreboard and posters all over the field acknowledged his comeback. Tears welled in my eyes as I ran my sprints and watched the crowd response.

When he took the mound in the top of the first inning, an incredible standing ovation made him cry. I cried right along with him. I prayed silently, *Lord, look how awesome you are. Who would have believed this? Thanks for letting me be part of it.*

Dave's first pitch was a strike, and the crowd went crazy again. Until they removed him from the game in the seventh inning, he was throwing like Sandy Koufax. Dave was a better-than-average pitcher, but no superstar. Except for that night. He was virtually untouchable. It was awesome.

As he left the mound, the stands erupted one more time. It was my biggest thrill in baseball.

Five days later he was scheduled to start in Montreal. Before that game, I asked him how he felt and he told me he felt whole again. He was excited that his arm had recovered just like it used to. Dave pitched well during the first five innings, but when we came in to hit at the top of the sixth he was feeling his arm.

I said, "You all right?"

"Ah," he said, "it's just a little tight."

"Could God be giving you a sign that you need to come out for now?"

"No, it's just a little fatigue."

In the bottom of the inning, with Tim Raines at the plate, Dave threw a pitch and I—along with just about everybody else in that stadium—heard a loud crack as Dave went down like a rag doll.

My heart sank. I didn't know what had broken, but it was as ugly a thing as I've seen on the ball field.

When we got in to hit in the top of the next inning, I hurried into the clubhouse. Dave was lying there, talking with the baseball chapel coordinator in Canada.

I asked Dave how he was doing. "Bugsy," he said, "I'm in pain."

As they wheeled him into the ambulance, he said, "Isn't God wonderful to allow me to pitch one more time?" He got the win for that game, the last he would ever pitch. It was something I'll never forget.

Dave eventually had to have his pitching arm removed to stop the spread of cancer. He now has a wonderful ministry of encouragement to other suffering people. I am fortunate to have him as a dear, lifelong friend.

The Cubs won the National League East that year, so we would play them for the right to go to the World Series. At first I thought it would be fun to go back to the area where I grew up, but it became a big hassle. Everybody I knew, and many I didn't, thought I was their hope for getting tickets. I spent so much time sorting the requests out and refereeing a little feud between my mother and my wife that I was unable to focus on and enjoy the play-offs. Some day I'd love to be able to play in the postseason without having all the other stuff to worry about.

My mother and my wife had been having trouble getting along for several years. It was hard for Mom to accept that there was a new love in my life who deserved my prime attention. The time finally came when I told my mother that she had better not make me choose, because I would have to choose Eveline.

After that, things were a lot smoother.

In the 1989 National League Championship Series, we beat the Cubs four games to one. We were excited about the World Series, but we never got on track.

The Oakland Athletics, a hugely powerful ball club, had been humiliated the year before by Orel Hershiser and the Dodgers, losing the Series in five games after having been highly favored.

Now they were focused and ready for revenge. We lost the first two games in Oakland and then the Series moved to Candlestick Park in San Francisco.

Eveline should have known something was wrong when she found herself riding in a black Volvo toward Candlestick Park for a World Series game. She was with three women: Jan Dravecky, Kathy Garrelts, and Jennie Hammaker. She had not known those three when she had her dream three years before.

Just about everybody close to me was in that stadium as I was running my wind sprints before the game. When the earthquake hit, I didn't know what had happened at first. The ground was shifting underneath me, as if I were drunk and stumbling. It sounded like everyone in the stands had begun stomping their feet, or as if a train were rumbling past. When a generator blew out and the lights went off, I nearly fell.

Eveline had been in line for an elevator with Kathy Garrelts, about to go up to their seats. When everything began to shake, Kathy yelled, "It's an earthquake!" and they got out of line. A well-known Oakland player nearly knocked Eveline down, rushing past her. All I could think of was getting my family and friends out of the stands. If the stadium had fallen, I would have lost everybody close to me except my kids. At that point I didn't know if they were safe either. Who knew how widespread this earthquake was?

My sister had left her infant son, Matthew, with a babysitter not far away, and she recalls the hours between the earthquake and reuniting with her child as the most horrible period of her life. There was no communication, no way to find out how our loved ones were doing. All we could do was get out of that stadium, get on the freeway, and spend four hours traveling to places that normally took only a half hour to drive.

That earthquake, which has been well-documented, reminded me again how insignificant baseball was. If we had been allowed to vote, I would have conceded the World Series to the Athletics and gone home. People had been killed in this thing. A double-decker highway had collapsed and entombed dozens of people. Who cared who won the World Series?

The Athletics apparently cared. While we tried to help the victims of the earthquake, the Athletics went to their training facility and worked out. When the Series resumed, they dispatched us easily twice and swept the Series.

The whole thing left a bad taste in my mouth. I felt as if we'd all been cheated out of a real World Series. That's one of the reasons I'm still playing. I want one more shot at it.

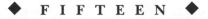

FIFTEEN

FINALLY
A DODGER

I had a solid three-year stint with the San Francisco Giants, and Eveline and I made more friendships that would stand the test of time. I led the National League in runs scored during my first year there, was the toughest hitter in the National League to double up my second year, and tied a major-league record for outfielders my third year by not hitting into a double play all season. In 1990 I tied for the league lead in hits with 192, and wound up hitting .309.

Life is much more than baseball, of course, but baseball has been my livelihood. I thought I had established in three years that I could do in the National League what I had done in the American League. That should have set me up for a comfortable, long-term contract.

The general manager of the Giants, Al Rosen, had been a great player in his own right back in the fifties with the Cleveland Indians. I liked most of what he had done with the Giants, and out of all the men I'd worked for in baseball, I respected Al the most.

He was like a father figure to me. I looked forward to what he and Dick Moss and I might be able to work out.

Because I was a run-producing lead-off man, sort of a Rickey Henderson without the power, it was generally considered that Rickey and I were numbers one and two in the pecking order for new-look free agents. Rickey had just signed a three-year deal for twelve million dollars, so I told Dick, "Try to get me eleven million."

I know those numbers sound astronomical—and they are—but dollars in professional sports are all relative. Everything starts with the top guy and goes down incrementally and chronologically from there. I saw Rickey Henderson above me at twelve million and I saw the Giants sign to a three-year deal at ten million dollars a pitcher who had a winning percentage of about .500. While a case can certainly be made that no one on earth is worth that kind of money for doing anything, it made sense to me that I certainly fit in somewhere between Rickey Henderson and a .500 pitcher.

Dick Moss reported that in his initial conversation about me with Al Rosen, Al said, "Will (Clark), Kevin (Mitchell), and Brett carry our ball club." Mitchell was an all-star slugger who had been MVP, and Clark was a young superstar. Both had recently signed contracts for fifteen million.

Dick told Al, "Just get us something comparable for Butler."

Of course, Dick was using that as a negotiating ploy, because he knew I would settle for eleven. He was doing what he was supposed to do, trying to get me the best deal he could. We figured Al would think it over, crunch some numbers, and come back with a counteroffer in the ten million range. Dick would tell him that eleven would get the deal done, and that would be that. Not so.

Eveline and I were at the winter meetings when I got a phone call from the Giants. It was the traveling secretary. He said, "Brett, Al Rosen's on the phone for you."

It was unusual for Al to talk directly to me during contract negotiations, but I thought, *Great! I'll talk to Al. We'll have this thing done in five minutes.*

Al, my dear friend, sounded distant. He was polite and cordial, but not the same old Al. "Brett," he said, "uh, you know, sometimes money changes things and changes people. I hate to be the bearer of bad news."

"What's up, Al?"

"Well, Brett, we're not going to be able to tender you a contract."

Eveline, who had been listening in, turned away and broke into tears. She was crushed. The Giants had become our team. We loved them. We wanted to stay.

"What do you mean?"

"You wanted fifteen million, and we can't do that."

"No, I didn't! I didn't want fifteen million. Did Dick say that?"

"That's the impression I got. We've had to go another direction here, so we're not offering you a contract."

By the time I hung up, I was crying too. Dick Moss called a few minutes later. "What in the world happened?" I demanded.

"The Giants just signed Willie McGee an hour ago for 13.9 million."

"Dick, they could have gotten me for eleven, almost three million dollars less. You know they wanted me. How could this happen?"

Dick tried to explain that it was a misunderstanding. He was just negotiating, but Rosen thought we had dug in our heels at the same figure Will Clark and Kevin Mitchell went for. I was mad at everybody. Mad at Al for misunderstanding. Mad at Dick for not making it clearer.

I sat there stewing. *Fine,* I thought. *I can't believe they offered me one contract and nothing else.*

Now I was determined to get back to Atlanta. I called one of my best friends, Lowery Robinson, whom I had met in the minors and had become close to over the years. He had played semipro ball with Stan Kasten, president of the Braves. I told Lowery, "You can tell Stan for me that I want to come back home. I want to play in the town where I live, and I'll sign for nine million dollars for three years right now."

So began a series of phone calls between Lowery and Stan and then Lowery and me while I tried to work out a deal on my own. Not knowing what might happen in Atlanta, I also let the general manager of the Dodgers, Fred Claire, know I was available.

Lowery called to let me know of his conversation with Stan Kasten.

"Stan is offering 6.8 million for three years," he said.

"That's insulting, Lowery."

"Tell me about it, Brett. I told him you were a man of your word and that if he would commit to nine million, you would do it right now." Lowery had also informed Kasten that I was talking with the Dodgers.

Fred Claire called me back. "We'll make the first offer," he said.

"Three years, three million a year, one million for signing. That's three years, ten million. Are you a Dodger?"

"I'll call you back," I said. I hung up and told Eveline. "Fred just offered us ten million dollars to play in Los Angeles."

"Well," she said, "did you tell him yes?"

"No. I just don't know. I want to play in Atlanta, but I also want to play in Los Angeles. As a kid my dream was to play in L.A."

"You've got to make that choice," Eveline said.

I called Lowery. "Call Stan Kasten back and tell him the Dodgers have offered me ten million for three years, but I'll sign right now for nine to come home to Atlanta. If I don't hear back, I'm gonna sign with the Dodgers in about twenty minutes."

A few minutes later Lowery called me back. "Stan says he doesn't want to dicker with the Dodgers. I told him he doesn't have to. I told him what you said."

That proved to me that Stan Kasten wasn't serious. He knew I would have played in Atlanta for less than I was being offered in L.A., but he didn't really want to pay more than the original 6.8 million. In the end, he told the press that I had every chance to sign with the Braves but didn't give them a chance to sign me. The headlines in Atlanta the next day said I had taken the money and run. Meanwhile, the San Francisco papers were saying virtually the same thing, that I had demanded top dollar and went elsewhere to find it.

I know it's hard to be sympathetic with somebody who has to "settle" for "just" ten million dollars to play baseball, but it was very painful to be treated that way in the press. I love the game, I respect the game, and I play for the fans. The last thing I wanted was for it to appear that my career was all about money, because it's not.

I had made the mistake of telling San Francisco reporters how excited I was to be going to the Dodgers. I said I had been born in L.A. and had been a Dodger fan as a child. Needless to say, that didn't go down well with my former Giant teammates, and some of them said so in print. I *was* excited to be a Dodger. But talking about it that way just made me look worse to the San Francisco fans, and they let me know it the first time they saw me in a Dodger uniform.

Meanwhile, in February of 1991, Eveline and I went to L.A. to look for a house. We knew we would be there for a few years, at least three, and while we weren't going to give up our main home in Atlanta, we needed a place for the family in California.

It should have been a fun, exciting time, and it started that way. When you're making more money than ever and breaking in fresh with the best organization in baseball, it can be an exciting time. Somehow, though, the tension of it all got to us. We were staying in a hotel while house hunting when I heard from my mother. She wanted to come stay with us and be there for opening day in April. I casually mentioned that to Eveline.

Her first reaction was, "We don't have a place yet. Why doesn't she stay with one of her sisters?"

"And why shouldn't she stay with us?"

"Brett! We just got here. We just started looking for a house. We don't even know where we're going to live. Your mother has fifty relatives in this area. Let her stay with one of them."

I was mad. "Well, what about what I want?"

"What about what *you* want!?" Eveline said. "What about what *I* want? You'll be getting on a nice charter plane to Vero Beach, Florida, for spring training soon. I'll be left with taking the kids out of school, supervising a move, unpacking, and all that. How can you start obligating me to houseguests when we don't even have a house yet?"

Now it was time to dig in my heels. "Well, she's staying with us and that's all there is to it."

"So I have no say in the matter? You don't care what I want?"

All of a sudden I was screaming, and I can scream. I was at the top of my lungs when Eveline said, "People are gonna hear—"

"They don't know who I am. They don't know who's in this room. And I don't care if they do hear. What are you talking about, what *you* want? I've given you everything you could ever want!"

Eveline was so scared she thought I was going to hit her, so she slipped past me and locked herself in the bathroom. I banged on the door and screamed even louder. She wouldn't let me in. I yelled, "Let me in!"

"Get out of here!"

Finally, I calmed down a little. I said, "Let's talk about this."

"No!"

I stormed out of the hotel room and walked around till I calmed down and could pray. *Lord, how could I lose my temper like that? Help me control myself.*

Eveline remembers: "I heard Brett leave the room and had no idea where he was going. I decided to call Lowery Robinson in

Atlanta and tell him my husband was being a jerk. I wanted Lowery to come to L.A. and fly home with me. His wife, Vicki, is one of my best friends, and I knew I could talk to her. But before I could make the call, Brett came back."

I was ready to apologize, but Eveline would have none of it. She told me to get out of her face, and I got mad all over again. "Why don't you want my mother to come and stay with us?" I demanded.

"Brett, that is not the issue! It's just too much to ask right now. We don't even know where we're going to be." And soon we were yelling at each other again.

Part of our misunderstanding stemmed from growing up in different kinds of families. My family is so close and loving, we take for granted that we'll be part of each other's lives. We think nothing of showing up on each other's doorsteps and assuming we'll be welcome to stay. Eveline's family is more formal and makes plans long in advance.

My family has also always been obvious about the fact that I belong to them and they belong to me. Eveline was mortified the first time she went to one of my games with my family. They were all wearing shirts that said they were Brett Butler's mother or sister or brother. They even had a shirt for her saying she was Brett Butler's wife. She refused to wear it, and that didn't sit well with them.

Later, some of the other players' wives overheard my mother talking about Eveline, saying she was money-hungry and that she cared more about herself than about my family. Apparently my mother complained that Eveline kept the best seats for herself and urged me not to spend money on my family. Of course that wasn't true, and such gossip should not have been shared with Eveline anyway, but it contributed to a power struggle that lasted much too long.

For the rest of that house-hunting week, Eveline and I were cordial to each other, but distant. Somehow we found a house and made all the arrangements while barely speaking to each other. The flight home was cold and uncomfortable, as were the next several days. My spiritual life was shot. I had been inconsistent in my prayer and Bible reading, and now there was this horrible argument with Eveline.

I began to humble myself before the Lord. Just about the time I would get to the point where I was willing to concede that I had overreacted to my wife, I would get tired of her treatment of me and start thinking about divorce. I was ashamed that thought was even running through my head, but I told myself, *I don't have to take this kind of treatment.*

At one point I said, "You know, every time you cry, I cave in."

Eveline immediately wiped her tears and said flatly, "Then you will never see me cry again."

For several days she hid her tears from me, though I knew she was as upset as I was.

Ironically, we kept our long-ago pledge to say "I love you" to each other before falling off to sleep each night. We said it reluctantly and grudgingly, but we both said it.

Finally, one night, about a week after we had begun that fight, I was sitting on the edge of the bed and saw Eveline in the bathroom wiping her eyes. I prayed silently, *Lord, what kind of a man am I?*

He seemed to impress upon me the question, *Other than me, what's the most important thing in your life?*

I said, *It's Eveline.* I walked into the bathroom. She was facing the mirror.

"Turn around," I said. She turned reluctantly. I knelt before her. "Honey," I said, "forgive me. I honestly believe Satan is trying to take away our peace and joy." I wrapped my arms around her legs and said, "Eveline, I love you with all my heart, and I don't ever want us to be like this again. Please forgive me."

She pulled me up and we embraced. "It's not that I don't want your mother there, you know," she said. "It's just that we didn't have a place to live yet."

And that was the end of it. We never want to fight like that again.

It didn't take long for us to reconcile. Soon we were excited again and looking forward to life with a new team. Ironically, come April, the Dodgers would open their season in San Francisco, not L.A. I had no idea what kind of a reception to expect. Or maybe I did.

EMBRACING
L.A.

Most of my relatives on both sides of the family live in California. My mother's oldest sister—my Aunt Edie—and my mother's younger brother—my Uncle John—were die-hard Dodger fans. In fact, when John was little he won a contest to be batboy for the Dodgers. I can still remember going to his house and seeing his Dodger batboy uniform. He had pictures of Sandy Koufax and Don Drysdale on his wall.

As a kid, I used to think being batboy for the Dodgers would be awesome. As a big leaguer, I was thrilled the first time I put on my uniform in the L.A. clubhouse. I looked down at the emblem on my chest and whispered, "The Dodgers."

When I signed with them as a player, it was like the bow on top of a gift-wrapped package. It was a present for my entire family. It always made me feel wonderful because they were so proud of me. They had tried to make all my games in San Diego, San Francisco, and L.A. when I was in the National League. They watched me in Oakland and Anaheim when I was in the American League. Now there would be eighty-one games a year in Los Angeles alone and several more in San Diego and San Francisco.

I was still devastated that my reputation had been tarnished in Atlanta and San Francisco by the way the contract negotiations had turned out. It was only fitting that we should open in San Francisco against the team I had just left. This was an appearance I needed to get behind me.

When I walked out on the field for batting practice, there was no question how the San Francisco fans felt. They shouted, "Traitor! You're no good! Butler, you ____!''

I knew the negative things that had happened were not all my doing. I had truly wanted to stay in San Francisco. It was a misunderstanding. But now I was a Dodger. I had always wanted to be one, and I was glad I now was. I couldn't go back and change anything.

In the clubhouse changing for the game, I decided there were people out there who would boo me and people out there who wouldn't. I also knew it was time to sever the relationship with San Francisco.

Some of my new teammates asked me what I was going to do. I said, "You know, when they announce the starting lineups, I'm gonna hug Tommy Lasorda.''

It's traditional on opening day to have the teams line up on the foul lines, just like in the All-Star Game or the World Series. The manager comes out first, then the players jog out as they are announced and shake hands or slap hands as they line up.

I went to Tommy's office. "Skip,'' I said, "just so you won't be surprised, when the starting lineup is announced, I'm gonna give you a big hug in front of all these San Francisco fans.''

Tommy roared. He thought that was a great idea. "I'll be ready,'' he said.

I was booed from the minute my number was announced, and the roar became deafening as I jogged out toward Tommy. When I embraced him, the place went ballistic. I was definitely a Dodger now.

As I waited in the on-deck circle for my first at bat, I ignored the derision of the fans and looked up into the box where Al Rosen sat. I caught his eye and tipped my cap to him. Some might have thought I was being sarcastic, but I wasn't, and he knew it. I made the gesture to thank him for the good years, and for the relationship we had before everything went sour. I still say he's one of the best.

At the end of that season, he would seek me out and tap me on the shoulder. When I turned around he said, "Brett, I need to tell you, not a day goes by that I don't think about what happened. I was known as a great player and I think I've done a pretty good job as a general manager, but this was one where I let my ego get in the way."

When Al finally retired, I called to tell him, "Baseball's going to miss a good man."

I still have great admiration for him. Losing my contract deal was just one of those dumb things that happen—a lack of communication. Of course I'm able to look back on it now and see that even in the mix-up, God had a plan. I don't know why he wanted me in L.A., or why he wouldn't let me play in Atlanta like I wanted to, but I have to keep trusting that he knows best.

Besides playing for what I considered the classiest organization in the big leagues, there were other reasons I loved playing in L.A. My grandmother Meredith Butler, my dad's mother, lived by herself in Newport. (My grandfather had died in 1974.) Whenever she wanted to come to a game, I left her a ticket. Sometimes she would let someone else drive her, and other times she would drive herself. I had visions of Mrs. Magoo careening down the expressways. But sometimes she wouldn't let me know in advance. She would just show up. I don't know how she did it, but somehow she would manipulate her way in. Grandma would tell them at the ticket window that her grandson, Brett Butler, had forgotten to leave her a ticket. I would come out for my first at bat and hear Grandma hollering from directly behind the dugout, "My grandson! There's my grandson!" She died in 1995 when she was 88, and I miss her surprise visits to see me play. She was exactly one day less than fifty years older than me.

One of the highlights of my career came during 1991, my first season with the Dodgers. At midseason, the All-Star teams were elected, and, as usual, I was in the running but did not make it. Despite what many people felt was a long career of solid .300-hitting years, I had never had one of those fabulous starts, a break-out first half that pushed me past all the glamour names that usually made the All-Star teams.

Once the teams were elected, the managers chose their reserves and extra pitchers. I won't lie to you, I would have loved to be an all-star. Who wouldn't? I didn't know how bad I wanted it until I thought the time had passed when the extras had been selected by their respective managers. I was pretty disappointed to have been passed over.

I was sitting in my hotel room when the phone rang.

"Brett, it's Tommy."

"Hey, Skip. What's up?"

"I just got a call from Lou Piniella." I held my breath. "He just picked you to be a reserve on the All-Star team."

I didn't know what to say.

"Congratulations, Bugsy. You there?"

"I'm here, Skip. Thanks a lot."

I hung up and the tears came. It still chokes me up to talk about it. I believe the Dodgers really talked me up for that role, and, of course, Lou Piniella will always have a special place in my heart.

I called Eveline. "I made it, Babe," I said. "I finally made one."

The All-Star Game was held at the Toronto Skydome that year, and the American League won for the fourth time in a row. I didn't play a role, but that wasn't what was most important to me. It was great to have been selected and to have the experience of going.

Eveline did a wonderful thing too. She recalls: "I had realized through that fight with Brett over the opening day fiasco with his mother, how important his mom was to him. I decided that if I loved Brett enough I would make sure I did things for her, rather than seeing her as someone who was stepping between us.

"I told Brett, 'I want your mom to go with us.' We got her a hotel room and involved her in everything. We sat together. I didn't even have my own mother come, which didn't make any points with her, but we got only two tickets and I thought, Brett may never make another All-Star team. His mom should be there.

"She and I had a great time at the game and she and Brett had a wonderful few days together. I was glad we did it."

One of the funniest things that happened while I was with the Dodgers actually came during the off-season, when I was back in Atlanta.

My friend Lowery Robinson and I were going to a business meeting, and his wife told him how important it was for him to dress up. He showed up in a suit. I was wearing ragged jeans and a casual shirt. He saw how I was dressed and said, "I'm gonna change too."

Lowery put on casual clothes and then both Vicki and Eveline got on us about how we looked. I tried to tell them we knew what we were doing, because this business meeting was with a friend, not somebody we had to worry about impressing. Still, they criticized us.

When we left, Vicki and Eveline went shopping. We were going to meet them later at a nice restaurant.

After our meeting, I told Lowery, "We need to teach our wives a lesson."

"How?"

"Come with me."

Lowery and I went to K-Mart and bought matching outfits. Our shoes, pants, belts, shirts, ties, and hats were all the same.

When we went to find the girls at the restaurant, the woman at the desk asked if we were with the band! I said, "No, we're not. We're meeting our wives here."

We walked in and saw the girls in the corner and started talking loud and stupid. I said, "Hey, Lowery! There's the girls! There they are!"

He said, "Yeah, it's them. Hey, girls! Here we are!"

Everybody was looking at us and Vicki and Eveline were embarrassed to death.

I don't know what Vicki says to Lowery now, but since then Eveline has never criticized me for how I dress.

It has not been all fun and games since I became a Dodger. If the San Francisco earthquake hadn't made us realize how fragile life was and how there were no guarantees, spring training of 1993 sure did.

Eveline remembers: "Brett was getting ready to go to the ballpark at Vero Beach when the news came over the radio that three Cleveland Indians had been in a boating accident the night before. Two of them, Tim Crews and Steve Olin, had died. I could hardly breathe. This was awful. We knew Tim and his wife, Laurie, well. He had been a Dodger before being traded to Cleveland after the previous season. Our daughters had played together.

"I dressed quickly to go to the ballpark with Brett, assuming that many other wives would be there too, as the news got around. On our way to the park, we were stopped at a drawbridge when Dave Hansen (one of our infielders) and his wife, Julie, pulled up behind us. Dave got out of the car and came over to talk to us. Julie and I were both crying. We wondered what Laurie was going to do. That's when I realized it would be foolish to have a false sense of security, to think that nothing could happen to our husbands. They may have been star athletes, but they were just like anybody else."

Tim's death really sobered me. I clearly remembered having shared Christ with him at the end of the season, just a few months earlier. "It's time to get your life in order," I told him. "You should turn your life over to Christ."

He said he heard me and he understood me. But he also said, "Brett, I'm only thirty-one years old. I've got my whole life in front of me. Maybe I'll do that later, but I'm going to enjoy life first."

I tried to tell him that he might not have as much time as he thought, but he pretty much told me that I should get off his case. I can only hope he thought it through some more and maybe made a decision before he was killed.

Having a good 1993 and a great first half of 1994, I felt especially blessed. People were saying I was one of the most consistent hitters in baseball, always hitting around .300 and producing a lot of runs. I was enjoying the game and my family and my faith more than ever. Trouble was brewing, however.

In August 1994, major-league baseball ground to a halt. Having been the victims of collusion in the past, the Players' Association now believed management was not dealing in good faith. The players struck, management dug in its heels, and the work stoppage went on and on. Eventually the season was ruined. Management talked some minor leaguers and amateurs into becoming replacement players, though team reps like me tried to urge the minor leaguers not to ruin their futures that way. I had been asked to do the same thing at the beginning of my career, and I refused. If these guys ever did make the big leagues legitimately, I knew they would suffer for having been scabs against the union.

The fans didn't understand either side of the issue, and I can hardly blame them. The players felt ownership came across as the good guys while we were portrayed as money-grubbing babies. Regardless, the whole thing went on way too long and baseball suffered. Fans lost respect for both the owners and the players, and I think we still suffer from that today. The 1994 season ended in the middle of the summer, and while we worked and worked, hoping to patch together some semblance of a postseason, it never happened. The year fizzled out, and everybody endured a September and an October without baseball.

I had probably the best start of my career that season, hitting .314 in 111 games. I knew I was making no points for myself with management now by being our team rep and fighting hard for the union, but I had to do what I felt was right. Maybe I was naive in thinking the owners would separate my union activities from my performance on the field. In retrospect, there was no maybe about it. I had been naive.

Fall 1994 and spring 1995 would be the busiest time of our lives as union reps. Everybody knew that both sides had to give somewhere, so we could bring baseball back for the fans and for ourselves.

In October 1994, my sister, Bev, called and said my mother had to go into the hospital so doctors could check a spot on her lung. Soon we had the report. Lung cancer. I flew to Chicago and stayed at Beverly's place in Lake Zurich. I was with my mother in the hospital when they removed part of her lung. All I can remember from that period is flying to union meetings and being with my mother in the hospital.

During the baseball strike the only thing discussed on the sports talk shows was deciding whom to blame. Eveline even called in once to defend the players' position when she thought commentators were being unfair. She knew I would be upset, but she felt she had to do it. The way our reputations were being tarnished seemed so unfair.

I had played through my option year on my original Dodger deal, so once players and management finally agreed to go back to baseball, it was time to renegotiate. Dick Moss had tentatively worked out an agreement that would see me play one more year for the Dodgers for 3.5 million. That sounded fair to me, and I assumed in due time the deal would be closed. Then I heard from Dick. The news hit me much the same way the Al Rosen phone call had hit me in 1990.

"The Dodgers are withdrawing their offer, Brett."

"They're what?"

"They're going with the kids."

"The kids? What does that mean? I hit .314 for them. What do they want? You're telling me I hit .314 and they don't want me?"

"Brett, you know exactly what's going on here."

I paused. "My union work?"

"What do you think?"

I was incensed, and I had a right to be. Though it had been a strike-shortened season, it had been one of my best. This made no sense. I went to see Peter O'Malley, owner of the Dodgers.

O'Malley is a good man. He cares about people. I didn't agree with his decision, and I can't say I believe everything he told me. But he's still a classy guy.

I asked him point blank, "Why, Peter? We had a tentative contract on the table for 3.5 million, and the only reason I can think of that you'd withdraw it is my involvement with the union."

"No, Brett," he said, "it was a business thing."

"You can't afford the 3.5 million? What if I told you I'd play for the minimum? I'll play for $109,000."

"Now, Brett, don't be rash. We've just decided to go with the kids."

"Just so I have this straight," I said, "you're telling me it's a business decision, even though I'll play for $109,000. You've decided to go with the youth movement and I'll just have to take your word that it's not my involvement with the union."

In spite of what he said, I knew it was my union work. There was no other explanation for it. I asked Dick to put out some feelers and find out who wanted me at the current market rates.

Several clubs said they were "upset" about what was being done to punish me, but I got no offers.

I heard through the grapevine that Fred Wilpon, owner of the New York Mets, thought I was being treated harshly. But when his general manager, Joe McIlvaine called, he offered me only $500,000 for one year.

That was insulting. Other players, statistically not at my level, were being offered much more. I was so mad I was ready to retire. If I didn't get what I believed was appropriate compensation, why did I need the grief anymore?

The next morning I woke to a jangling phone. It was John Franco, Bret Saberhagen, and Dallas Green—two pitchers and the manager of the New York Mets.

Dallas said, "We know what they're doin' to ya, Brett. We'd like you to come here. We sure could use you."

We spoke for several minutes, and I started to feel pretty good. It was nice to be wanted. Dallas said he would have Fred Wilpon call me. I looked forward to that. I wanted to give him a piece of my mind.

I mean, I would love to play on a team where I was wanted, but I wasn't about to go there for $500,000. I hoped he would call soon.

A BAD STRETCH BEGINS

When Fred Wilpon called, I was ready for him. I said, "Before you say anything, Mr. Wilpon, I need you to know I've been fed up with this whole thing, and I'm hurting. Let me just tell you I'm offended by the offer you made. Andre Dawson's probably one of the greatest players in the game and maybe even a Hall of Famer, but he's had all those knee surgeries and he can hardly walk. They offered him $500,000. I hit .314 last year. I don't need to play for 3.5 million, but I will tell you now, I have a figure in mind that I believe is below market value, but it's reasonable. If I don't get that figure, I'm retiring. I don't need this."

Wilpon told me that Joe McIlvaine would call Dick Moss the next day. "We'll figure something out. I just don't like what they're doing to you."

I hadn't told him the figure I had in mind of course, but I called Dick Moss immediately. "Dick, the number is two million. I don't care what Joe offers; it's two million. Either he's going to give me that or I'm done."

Later, Dick told me how it went. He called Joe McIlvaine, who said he had talked to Fred Wilpon, and that the Mets "could give him a million plus incentives, which would probably get him up to two million or so."

Dick told Joe, "No, you're making this too difficult. The figure is two million. If not, he's going to retire. It's as simple as that."

"Well," Joe said, "we can't do that."

"Fine, then he's going to retire."

"Let me try to get hold of Fred again."

"Okay."

Ten minutes later, the deal was done. I still felt used and abused by baseball in general, but I was glad to be going to a team where I could contribute.

I didn't know that the baseball strike, my union involvement, my jilting by the Dodgers, and accepting less than market value to play for the Mets signaled the start of a bad stretch for me. I never thought of life in those terms. I took it one day at a time and tried to stay close to God.

The first time the Mets played the Dodgers in spring training, I felt out of sorts. It was as if I had the wrong uniform on.

Just a few days before spring training was over, I got a call in the middle of the night from Eveline, who had heard from my sister, Beverly. "Mom's had a seizure," she said. Immediately I feared the worst. The cancer had gone to her brain. That was the only explanation for a seizure.

I called Jay Horowitz, the Mets' traveling secretary, and apologized for waking him up. "Jay," I said, "in the morning let Dallas know that I had to leave. My mother's had a seizure and I've got to go home."

Jay must have called Dallas immediately. He called me at two, before I left. He said, "Go. Do what you've got to do."

When I got back to Illinois I got the awful news. It was a brain tumor. She was given six months to a year to live. Mom was not the type you kept such news from. Her response? "If Jesus had to suffer a little bit, I guess I can too." I was inspired by how solid she was in her faith, even at the worst hour of her life.

I offered to stay with my mother, but she said, "You can't do much for me now. Just go and make me proud of you."

So I rejoined the team, always dreading a phone call that might bring the bad news. I never let personal problems influence my performance, so I won't blame my mediocre batting start on that. I had heard all the horror stories about playing in New York. The city was supposed to be cold and indifferent, the press overwhelming and negative. It was said the sportswriters there could chew you up and spit you out.

I actually found I enjoyed the place. It was wonderful to get to know the town, the restaurants, the fans, the workers at the park, the cops. Everybody was great to me.

The fans were wonderful until one night in June when I played terrible and got booed. I had two hits bounce off my glove. One was ruled an error, but the fans thought I should have caught them both, and I probably should have. At the plate I was 0-for-5 with two, maybe three strikeouts. I was just awful. The fans let me have it.

After the game I sat slumped before my locker, and here came the press. I was used to L.A. where there were a lot of people in the locker room, but now there were about thirty reporters from the New York press. Somebody shoved a microphone in my face and said, "You know, Brett, the fans in New York are cynical."

There was a setup if I ever heard one. If I agreed, it would be my quote and the headlines the next day would say I accused the fans of being cynical. I always believed that if you have a bad game you should be professional about it. You stand in the front of the press when you're 4-for-4, and you stand there when you've had an 0-for also. So how do I answer a question that suggests New York fans are cynical?

I said, "You know what? That might be so. But when the New York Mets signed me, they signed an all-star center fielder who's supposed to catch the ball and a lead-off man who's supposed to get on base and set the table. I feel bad for Bill (Pulsipher, who had made his major-league pitching debut that night). He gave up only one run, but the other four or five were my fault. And I sure stunk today at the plate. But I can guarantee you guys one thing— every day Brett Butler goes out on the field he's going to give you everything he has. I might be brutal that day, but you'll have gotten all I've got to give. If I have another day like this, you guys come back here, 'cause I'll be standing here. Just don't blame it on the fans. They expect me to go out there and do my job."

That was it. It was over. They walked away and I sat back down. Our third-base coach, Mike Cubbage, came over. "Brett, that's the first time in years I've heard a player say, 'It was my fault, I lost the ballgame.' I just want you to know how refreshing that was."

I performed below par all the way into July. I was hitting about .250, and one day I came to the ballpark and found I was not in the lineup. I thought, *Okay, no big deal.* The next day I came in and I still wasn't in the lineup. Now I wanted to know what was going on.

I had enjoyed playing for Dallas Green so far. He's a mountain of a man, a former pitcher, and a straight shooter. He always told the ball club that if any of us had anything to say, we should come in to see him. It was a typical manager's open door policy. The younger guys are usually too intimidated to take him up on it, but I sure wasn't. I knocked on his door.

When he invited me in and offered me a chair, I sat down and started in. "What the heck is going on?"

Dallas responded quickly. "I don't need that prima donna _____. I never had to tell Larry Bowa what I was doing. I never had to tell Mike Schmidt what I was doing."

I said, "Wait a second, Dallas. I simply asked you a question. You said your door is always open. I'm not one of the kids. All I'm trying to figure out is what's going on. If you're not going to play me every day, tell me what my role is so I can help the young guys, and when the season's over I'll be gone. But don't sit here and yell at me. I'm not Schmidt or Bowa, I'm Butler. I'm just asking your opinion. What's going on?"

Dallas wasn't used to being spoken to that forthrightly, but I think he respected it. "First of all," he said, "against lefties you're hitting about a buck thirty-five."

I nodded. "You're right."

"If you were hitting .300, you wouldn't be in here, would you?"

"Right again, but my stats show that if I get five hundred plate appearances I'm gonna hit you .300. You know that. So are you gonna play me? Just let me know what my role is. I'll be happy to help the kids. I'm not here to take your job. I'm here to help you."

Then Dallas made a mistake, because I'm very opinionated. He said, "Put yourself in my position—"

I lost it. "I have, Dallas, and frankly your communications skills stink. You've got guys out there who are scared to death of you because you're six-foot-five and weigh two hundred and fifty pounds, and you're intimidating as all get-out. It's okay to kick some of these kids, but you've got to coddle some of them too. You've got sons. You know how it is."

Dallas interrupted me. "Aw, I don't want to hear that. I've been hearing that for forty years."

"Well, Dallas, if you've heard it for forty years, maybe there's something to it. I understand the game. I'm not intimidated by you. But you might want to go a little easy on some of these younger guys."

"I'll tell you what, Butler. I'm not gonna play you today, and I'm not gonna play you tomorrow. Then I'll play your butt off."

"Fair enough."

Two days later I came in early for a Bible study and one of the pitchers said, "You said something to Green, didn't you?"

"Why?"

"Because he called us all in and started telling us he was there to support us and help us and all that."

I just smiled.

In the middle of July, I saw the softer side of Dallas Green. We headed into Chicago for a series against the Cubs, and I looked forward to getting back home. My mother had taken a turn for the worse, and I found out she wanted to come to the games anyway. That sounded impossible, but if that's what she wanted, that's what we wanted for her.

I must have been pressing in Chicago through the years, because I had never hit well there. I put that out of my mind for this trip, though, because I wanted my mom to see me play one last time.

Through a family friend who worked for the Cubs, we arranged for a luxury box for my mother. We stationed her there in her wheelchair, oxygen tubes running to her nose, one of her arms twitching uncontrollably. I mentioned to umpire Randy Marsh that my mother, who didn't have long to live, was at the game. He said, "Where is she?" I pointed her out. Randy waved until he got her attention and saluted her. She waved back. I was moved by his gesture.

Having my mother there must have inspired me, because I took a .263 average into that series, got four hits in each of the three games, and raised my season average to .290. Two weeks later I had another four-hit game.

Best of all for me, though, was July 20, the third of that three-game set in Chicago. We were way ahead in the seventh inning when I got my fourth hit. After I crossed the plate and high-fived everyone, I trotted to the dugout where Dallas Green met me. "You're done," he said. "Go get dressed and spend the rest of the time with your mom."

"Really, Skip?"

"Get going."

Sitting up in a box with my mother in Wrigley Field and watching the end of that game is something I'll never forget. It was the best gift Dallas could give me.

As the end neared for Mom, she stayed in a hospital bed at Beverly's home. My grandmother and my Aunt Edie flew back from California and stayed with my mother. When my aunt finally said she needed to get back to her job because she needed the money, I said, "Forget it. You stay here. You've been working there for thirty-some years, so you can call your boss and tell him what's going on. I'll give you the money you need, but please stay with Mother."

Eveline brought the kids up from Atlanta and I met them in Chicago, so we could go visit Mom as a family. The last time my kids had seen her was during the winter when she came to Grandparents' Day at school. She had gone to each of their classes and had her picture taken with them. They each had those pictures on their nightstands. Now, when they walked into her room, they recoiled. Mom's hair was thinning and she was moon-faced from all the steroids and medication. She didn't look like herself even to me. At first the kids didn't want to get close to her. I said, "That's Grandma. She doesn't look the same, but that's her." I finally persuaded them to give her a hug, but it made them all cry. I kissed her on the forehead and lay next to her in the bed and told her I loved her.

She seemed to worsen every day. At one point I told her, "Mom, if you want, you can give up. Go ahead. I'll take care of Ben and Beverly. We'll be all right. You go be with Dad."

When we left, she was still hanging in there. I called every day for an update and talked to her a little bit.

The Mets and I were in the dog days of August. My batting average was rising, but that was the last thing on my mind. Beverly told me she had begun sleeping in the same room with Mom. Often in the night Mother would sit up and shout, "No! I'm not ready! I'm not ready!"

"Mom," Beverly would ask, "are you all right?"

"Yeah. He's outside."

"Who's outside, Mom?"

"He's coming. He's outside." Needless to say, that really freaked out Beverly.

A couple of days went by and then Mom started talking about "him" being "downstairs, in the basement."

"Who, Mom? Who's down in the basement?"

"He's in the kitchen."

A few days later, "He's at the foot of my bed."

The Mets were in Philadelphia playing the Phillies when I was called to the phone. It was Beverly. "Brett, I think it's time."

"We're playing right now, and I couldn't get out tonight anyway. I'll finish the game and be there tomorrow. I'll call you after the game with details."

After the final inning, I rushed to the phone and called Beverly. "How's she doing?"

"She keeps saying, 'I can't go until Brett comes.' Her eyes are open right now. Do you want to talk to her?"

Beverly put the phone up to Mom's ear. I said, "Mom, I love you. It's Brett. I'll be there tomorrow, Mom. Hang in there."

All of a sudden I didn't hear anything. My sister got on the phone. "I think she quit breathing, Brett. Wait a second."

I waited.

"I think she just died. She's gone."

She had been alive when I started talking to her. It was as if I had given her permission to go.

The funeral was much like my father's. I saw all our relatives and friends and people I hadn't seen for years. After the funeral we planned to fly her out to California, to bury her in Glendora next to Dad. Eveline tried to explain to the kids. "We have to put Grandma on the plane and fly her out to California," she said.

Little Stefanie piped up, "*I'm* not sitting next to her!"

That was just the tension breaker we needed. What a great line for a kid.

My old buddy Mark Salzman, whom I had known since 1979 when I went to work for him one summer at a clothing store in the Chicago area, went with us to California. He planned to fly back to New York with me for a Mets home series against the Dodgers as Eveline flew back to Atlanta. After the burial, Mark and I dropped Eveline off at her gate and went on to ours. When we realized we had a couple of hours before our flight, I said, "Why don't we go have coffee with Eveline?"

We walked all the way back to her gate and I sat down next to her. She was reading the paper. I leaned real close like a weird stranger, and she turned to stare me down, suddenly realizing who I was.

"What are you doing over here?" she said. But before I could answer we heard an announcement.

"Paging Eveline Butler. Paging Eveline Butler. Please go to the nearest courtesy phone."

We had never been paged in our lives, so I wondered what was going on. It was my sister. She said my cousin Jimmy had called and said he had just read in the paper that I was going to get traded back to Los Angeles.

"Jimmy's a prankster," Eveline said. "He's just messing around."

But we sat there wondering if it could be true. Two Dodger outfielders had been hurt. Maybe there was something to this. I said, "I doubt it. Too much of a long shot."

Eveline said, "Well, if you get traded to the Dodgers, you'd better call me. I don't want to hear it on ESPN."

Mark and I flew to New York and the first thing I did when I got off the plane was buy a paper. Sure enough, it said the Brett Butler trade from the Mets back to the Dodgers might be done that day. I thought, *You've got to be kidding me! That would be awesome!*

Mark and I grabbed a cab and went straight to Shea Stadium.

Jay Horowitz, our traveling secretary, met me at the door. "What's happening, Jay," I said. "Is a trade really going to happen?"

"Brett," he said, "it happened fifteen minutes ago. You're going back to the Dodgers."

"I've got to go get my stuff," I said.

"We've already moved your stuff to the other side."

"Jay, are you kidding me? Am I going to play with the Dodgers against the Mets right here tonight?"

"You just might," he said.

I couldn't believe it.

It was fun for Mark, a longtime sports fan, to sit in on the whole thing. He got to talk to Fred Wilpon and Joe McIlvaine and several other Mets, including David Howard, their general counsel. David's a Christian, and we had become good friends.

People began kidding me. They said, "It's almost as if your mother got to heaven and told God you'd suffered enough and it was time to get you back to Los Angeles."

It was fun calling Eveline and breaking the news. We were both thrilled.

I walked into the visitor's clubhouse where the Dodgers were getting dressed. Chris Gwynn was the first player to greet me. He hollered out, "Bugsy! You're back!"

It was as if nothing had changed. I had been a New York Met for four months and ninety games, and now I was back with Los Angeles. Guys were hugging me and shaking my hand and telling me how great it was to have me back.

I approached David Wright, our clubhouse man, and said, "Dave, can I get my number back?"

"Well," he said, "you're going to have to ask the guy who's got it now."

He pointed to Chad Fonville, a rookie who had begun the season in Montreal and joined the Dodgers in my absence. I told Dave, "Just give me twelve or something close for now."

I was in the training room when Chad Fonville approached. "I hear you want your number back. You know, I broke in with this number. It's been good luck for me."

I said, "Hey, Chad, listen. I'm at the end of my career and you're at the beginning. If you feel like you need that number to succeed, that's fine. You're welcome to it. But let me tell you something. In Los Angeles I'm known as number twenty-two. It's gonna look strange with me running out there with number twelve, but if you feel like you have to have twenty-two, that's fine."

Bill Russell, who's now the manager of the Dodgers but then was the bench coach, said, "Hey, Bugsy, just take a couple of days."

"No," I said.

"You want to play tonight?"

"Yeah."

"You haven't played in, what is it, nine days?"

I said, "I want to play tonight."

"Okay."

I was out running sprints prior to the game when Raul Mondesi came up. "Bugsy? Where's your number? You're twenty-two, not twelve."

"Fonville doesn't want me to have it."

"I'll get it for you," Raul said.

I don't know what Raul said to him, but after the game, Fonville said, "Hey Brett, you can have your number. You deserve it."

Coming back to Dodger Stadium was a thrill too. I was met with welcoming posters and standing ovations. Unfortunately, that honeymoon wouldn't last long.

A TOUGH
YEAR

It was August 29, 1995, and I had been back with the Dodgers less than two full weeks. The problem was, I had not been with the Mets long enough for anyone, especially the press, to realize that I should no longer be considered a spokesman for the Dodgers. When the L.A. front office decided to promote to the big leagues a six-foot-five, two-hundred-fifty-pound, otherwise unassuming minor-leaguer named Mike Busch, controversy exploded.

Mike had been a replacement player—what some would have called a strikebreaker, a scab.

Let me set the record straight: I have nothing against Mike Busch, and I never did. I don't hold a grudge against replacement players. I disagree with them. I believe they're wrong. And I will stand behind my actions until the day I die.

As soon as it was announced that Busch would join the team, the Dodgers went ballistic. Milwaukee had tried to bring up a couple of former replacement players, and the team let management know they wouldn't even take the field. They ran those guys off pretty quick. It may have been a cruel thing to do to a couple of young ballplayers, but it kept tensions from elevating.

With my experience as a union rep, everybody came to me. Immediately I was in the middle of the controversy. Players were saying, "Bugsy, get this guy out of here. We don't want him."

We called a team meeting and asked Fred Claire to join us, but we didn't want Mike Busch there. We wanted management to know how we felt and that we were all in agreement. "Fred," I said, "we've got a problem. We don't want Busch here. We think he's a scab. It's going to be a bad situation."

Fred told us in no uncertain terms that the inmates don't run the asylum. We got the feeling it didn't matter what we thought or wanted. "The decision is mine," he said. "He's here and that's the way it is."

I said, "Fred, this is gonna tear our ball team apart. We're going down the stretch, trying to get in the play-offs, and this is gonna be a major distraction. This kid might be ready for the big leagues talent-wise, but you have no idea the ramifications of all this. I know what you're trying to do, but this isn't the way to do it."

I give Fred credit for having an open door, but he had made up his mind. He would have to live with the consequences.

Needless to say, we were not happy campers. Unfortunately for me, I had to take the heat for the situation because I was the union leader. And it just happened that the next person I ran into after our meeting with Fred was Bob Nightengale of the *Los Angeles Times*.

I've always tried to get along with reporters. I know they have a job to do. I don't run from them when I've had a bad game, and I always try to give them some positive comment about what went on. Bob's question that day was, "What do you think about Mike Busch being on the team?"

I feel I was later misquoted. What I should have said was that he wasn't really on the team and would never be part of the team.

But I tried to be diplomatic. I said, "Well, you've got twenty-five different people on this team and you'll get twenty-five different opinions. We're in uncharted waters. We don't know how people are going to react to this. We don't even know how they're going to respond in the stands or toward his wife."

That was noncommittal I thought. I didn't try to speak for anybody else. In fact, I didn't say everything that was on my own mind.

The next day Nightengale reported that I had called Busch a scab player and said the team was going to ostracize him and his wife. It made the headlines. I don't know when I've been angrier. I couldn't wait to get to the ballpark.

In baseball lingo, when you criticize somebody or put him down, it's called blowing someone up. As soon as I saw Bob Nightengale, I blew him up in front of everybody. "Bob! I cannot believe you did that to me. That's not what I said and you know it! You know what this is going to do, and it's your fault. Anything to get a story, right, Bob?"

That night the Dodgers were closing in on the end of August, still in the pennant race, and the stadium was full. As I waited to hit in the bottom of the first, the P.A. announcer said, "Leading off, playing center field, number twenty-two, Brett Butler!"

Boos rained down on me from fifty thousand people. I had never experienced anything like it. I mean, I had been booed before. The Giants fans booed me after the trade, but that was almost in fun, the way people get on each other when loyalties are traded. I was booed in New York when I had a bad game, but that was for sloppy play, and I deserved it. All of a sudden these people, my people, sounded as if they hated me.

Mike was being ostracized by the team, no question about that. He sat by himself on the bench, and no one talked to him. Tommy Lasorda put him in to pinch hit in the seventh inning, and he received a standing ovation. He probably felt more pressure than I had. When he struck out and walked back to the dugout, he received another standing ovation.

Overnight, I became the enemy. Self-righteous sportswriters wrote about how I claimed to be a Christian and yet treated a person that way. I knew something had to give.

For a couple of days tension was unbearable in the clubhouse. No one talked to Mike, and he moped around, just trying to get dressed and warm up and be ready when Tommy needed him. I decided to say something. I came in early and called him aside privately. I said, "Mike, you need to know what's happening here. This is not personal."

"Brett," he said, "nobody else will talk to me."

"I know," I said. "It isn't fair to you. You're being used. I'm being used. You've been put in an impossible situation. But let me tell you how the guys feel and why they all feel that way."

I tried to explain to him how we felt that the players who had gone before us had stood together. Sure, there's a lot of money in baseball and that can make players look selfish and greedy. But it wasn't that long ago that players had to work during the off-season to support their families. As recently as the 1960s, even a future Hall of Famer like Nolan Ryan went home to Texas and drove an oil truck to help make ends meet. When I broke into baseball in the early 1980s, my initial salary was $32,500. Just eight years before that, the minimum salary was $12,000. I tried to tell Mike that someone breaking the union, crossing the line, weakening the position of the players, offended everybody. It seemed like disrespect for the players who'd gone before us. We were trying to set the tone for future players.

I asked him, "When you decided to become a replacement player, did you think you wouldn't make it to the big leagues any other way?"

"That's what I thought," he said.

"You need to tell the team that. I don't know what difference it will make, but it's important they know that. Because if you thought you would make it on your own, you definitely should have stayed out. That's what I did in 1981. I was offered a chance to play when the big leaguers were on strike. But I didn't want to be known forever after that as a scab."

"The guys won't listen to me," Mike said.

"I'll call a team meeting. They'll listen."

Getting everybody together for a meeting with Mike Busch was not as easy as I thought, but we did finally have a closed-door session. Mike spoke his piece and the guys sat there silently.

"Mike," I said, "I appreciate your talking to us. I don't agree with what you've done, but thanks for explaining your side of it. I still believe you were put in an impossible situation with no chance to win. I can't tell you that if you had gotten a hit I would have shaken your hand, or if you'd gotten into a fight that I would have backed you up, but now that you've talked to us and you're wearing the Dodger uniform, you're my teammate. I don't know about the rest of you guys, but for as long as Mike Busch is a Dodger, I'm treating him like a teammate."

Later we had a press conference and I said virtually the same thing. That seemed to end the controversy, but it had been an ugly few days. I wouldn't care to go through it again.

A couple of days later Peter O'Malley called me into his office. "Brett," he said, "I just want to thank you. I believe you single-handedly kept our house from burning down. I appreciate it."

"You know, Peter, what happened was wrong."

To his credit, Mr. O'Malley said, "Well, the buck stops here. I'm the one who ultimately makes the final decision. But thanks for handling it in a professional manner."

I still had unfinished business. As the season wore on and we finally fell out of the pennant race during the last week or so, my relationship with Bob Nightengale nagged at me. We weren't speaking. I was still mad about being misquoted and suffering the public outcry, but I certainly hadn't helped the situation by blowing Bob up in front of everybody. I prayed about it, but didn't know what to do. I tried to push it from my mind. That would eventually prove impossible.

My contract for the 1995 season carried several incentive clauses, two of which carried large bonuses if I hit at least .300 and stole at least thirty-two bases. With one game left on the schedule against the Padres in San Diego, I was hitting .299 and had stolen thirty-one bases. I had hit .311 for the Mets but was hitting only about .275 for the Dodgers. That averaged out to just a tic under .300. In baseball parlance, I needed a knock and a bag.

While I was getting dressed for the game, Bill Russell came by. "You're not playing today," he said.

"Oh yes I am."

"Nah," he said, "we're gonna play the kids."

"Billy, you can't do this to me." I told him about my contract and where I stood. "I've got to play."

"Okay," he said. "Get in there and get your hit and your bag and then get out."

I led off the game, and Ken Caminiti was playing me deep at third. I couldn't resist the temptation to lay one down, but I bunted the first pitch foul. As the Padre pitcher wound up for the second pitch, Ken was still deep, so I tried it again. Another foul. Now I'm 0-2. I fouled off a pitch and here came a change-up. I sort of threw the bat at it, hit it off the end, and it scooted past Kenny at third. Now I was hitting .300. I stole second, Billy took me out of the game, and that was my season.

It had been a tough year: the Dodgers dumping me, my mother's diagnosis, her death, the trade back, and the replacement player fiasco. I had turned thirty-eight that June and though I had averaged over .295 for the last several seasons, I began to listen to those "experts" who had decided it might be time for me to think about hanging up the spikes.

I've always been grateful that my "weakness" is also my strength. Being small and light allowed me to continue playing the game like a young man. I felt healthy and strong and still loved baseball. No way I was ready to quit.

Meanwhile, my grandmother on my mother's side was diagnosed with leukemia. My grandmother on my father's side, the one who used to talk her way into Dodgers games without a ticket, developed Alzheimer's. She died that winter, and I wondered what more a person could go through. With hindsight, of course, I can see that was only the beginning.

Usually I love the off-season and the chance to spend uninterrupted time with Eveline and the kids. That was great during the winter of 1995–96, but I was still troubled by my estranged relationship with Bob Nightengale. He had written a brief retraction, but it ran on the back page and didn't really satisfy me. Still, I felt guilty about the way I had talked to him.

Eveline and I have always been grateful for what God has brought into our lives. We like to say that if God had come to us when we met and said, "Choose your lives, whatever you want, and you can have it," we would never have chosen anything as wonderful as the way it turned out. Even with everything we've gone through, we wouldn't have dreamed to ask for all we have received.

In January 1996, Eveline went to a women's conference with Indy Cesari. She recalls: "I had been really struggling with my walk with the Lord. During the past year I had been praying, *God, what do you want me to do? Where do you want me? Where's my commitment? I feel like I'm not contributing. I'm raising my kids, but am I supposed to be doing something else?*

"Still, I was afraid. I had known other people like the Dave Draveckys and the Steve Bedrosians who had learned the hard lesson that when you really give your life up to the Lord and release everything to him, you'd better watch out. You will go through deep water.

"I didn't want some major tragedy in our lives. I was arguing with God. I was saying, *Lord, why does something tragic have to happen? Can't I just go where you want me to go without having some awful thing come into our lives? I wouldn't want you to have to take one of my kids to make me committed to you. I can be committed without that.*

"At the women's conference I sat talking with Christine Burke (wife of former major-league pitcher Tim Burke), Jackie Kendle (an author and speaker), Indy, and Laura Rutledge (wife of football player Jeff Rutledge). At one point I said to them, 'I really feel God wants me to go to the next level, but I'm afraid. Can't I go there without something bad happening?'

"They all just sat there looking at me and shaking their heads slightly. I said, 'Come on, you guys, really. I want to be sold out and committed, but how do you get past the fear factor?'

"Their counsel to me was that there is no easy way to that next level with God. It's not automatic that bad things happen, but you must be willing to endure them. It might be the price you're expected to pay. In other words, there may be no easy way to get there from here."

That same month, I went to speak at a men's breakfast in Atlanta. Afterward a man came up to me and said, "You don't know me, but in my prayer time this morning I prayed for you, knowing you were going to speak today. I feel as if God told me to give you this."

He handed me a document five or six pages long. People do that to me a lot, so I simply thanked him and put it in my pocket.

When Eveline asked me how things went, I told her and showed her the document. "Did you read it?"

"No." I really had no intention of reading it. I had taken it only to be polite.

"Let me see it," Eveline said, "I'll read it."

"I found it very interesting," Eveline recalls. "An OB/GYN and pharmacist had developed a vitamin supplement after contracting a disease from a patient. He had done a lot of work with

T cells and the thymus gland, so he researched and developed a compound that seemed to help people with AIDS, hepatitis, MS, lupus, and different kinds of cancer. I wondered why God would have told that man to give Brett the information. I had a few friends with lupus and other diseases, so I copied it and gave it to them and put our copy up in my cabinet. I wouldn't think about it again for months."

Dick Moss had called the Dodgers to see if they wanted me back for another season. I assumed they did, but I had learned such assumptions were not always automatic.

They signed me to a one-year deal, and I looked forward to at least one more spring training. I still wanted to play on a World Series winner, and I thought we had a shot.

Two weeks before leaving for spring training 1996, I felt the tickle in my throat that would change my life. When Dr. Bob Gadlage laughed and told me I had "a kid's disease," I assumed I could put off worrying about it.

The first day of spring training I saw Bob Nightengale. "Bob," I said, "can I talk to you for a minute?"

We moved away from everybody else. "Bob, it's been bothering me all winter and I've just go to tell you. I'm a born-again Christian and believe that the sun is not supposed to go down without me making things right. I need your forgiveness for blowing you up in front of everybody. I thought what you did was wrong, but it was also wrong for me to do that to you. That's why I'm here. Forgive me."

"I forgive you, Brett. It's been bothering me all winter too."

From that point on, we were fine.

Then I started my great spring, starting fast and hitting well. Only my sore throat and fatigue kept me from fully concentrating on baseball.

FIGHTING BACK

Not two months later, I had left the ball club for a simple tonsillectomy, then learned I had cancer while suffering through my recuperation. Now I faced another surgery: the neck dissection that would determine my future.

Among the many friends and relatives who had gathered in the hospital to support me that day were Walt Wiley, my spiritual mentor, and his wife, Patti. Walt wins the award for the funniest line of the day. As I was being outfitted with my hospital gown, which proved typically revealing, Walt said, "That gives a whole new meaning to ICU!"

That was almost as funny as when I was being interviewed by an intern just before I was given the pre-op anesthetics. The young doctor asked, "Do you have any serious illnesses?"

I couldn't resist. I said, "You mean besides cancer?" Maybe that shouldn't have made everyone laugh, but it sure did.

Soon I was doped up and the last thing I remember before being wheeled out for the operation were those sad, worried faces of my loved ones.

Eveline picks up the story:

* * *

I walked with Brett as they wheeled him toward the operating room, and he kept insisting that I stay with him, that I be there when he woke up. I assured him I would be. By then I was fighting tears and trying to be strong for him. He knew I would tell him the truth and not try to play games. Finally we got to the point where I was not allowed to go further with him. That was a painful parting. This surgery was major, but it shouldn't be life-threatening and would be less painful than the tonsillectomy. Yet in these cases you never know if you'll see your husband again. He wanted to hang on to me. I wanted to hang on to him. But I had to let him go.

All I could think of was our oldest daughter, Abbi, crawling up into Brett's lap one evening. "Daddy," she said, "I don't want you to die. I pray to Jesus every night to give me your cancer because I know I could handle it. But I don't like to see you in pain."

Then there had come the days when Brett's emotions had started on a fatalistic roller coaster. He started talking about where he wanted to be buried and what kind of funeral he wanted. I didn't want to hear about it. Finally, I said, "You can just stop that right now! If you want to think about all that stuff, if you want to play it out in your mind, write it in a letter and seal it. If and when you die, I'll open it and I'll read it and I'll do everything you want. But I don't want to hear about it now."

We had traded personalities. If I was the pessimistic realist before, I was the optimist now. I would have a positive mental attitude about this whether he did or not. I knew he could beat this thing if he kept the right state of mind. I said, "You're a fighter, and you'd better fight."

After they took Brett into the operating room, I made my way back to the suite and to so many friends. By now there must have been about thirty people there. I was especially grateful for Vicki, Indy, and Suzanne. They were very sensitive to me. People were coming and going and I was trying to be polite to all of them. I greeted everyone and thanked them for coming and supporting us. A couple of times those three closest girlfriends took me by the arm and dragged me outside onto the huge balcony. "Listen," they said, "you are not here to be a social butterfly to all these people or to entertain them. If you need to be alone, we'll tell everyone to wait somewhere else."

"No, no, that's fine," I said. I didn't really want anyone to leave, but it did feel good to have those three constantly watching out for me.

About two hours into the operation, Dr. Bob came out to give us a status report. It seemed strange that everyone was there to hear it, but that's the way we had been handling it all along. He said Brett was doing fine and that Dr. Grist was encouraged by how things were going.

Lowery Robinson, who's always cutting up, decided to take it upon himself to go and check on Brett's progress. He talked a nurse into getting him a set of scrubs, and he went wandering around trying to find out whatever he could. I told him I drew the line at the operating room. He was not to go in there. We had so many doctors whose last name started with G, people started calling Lowery Robinson "Dr. Gobinson."

When it was finally all over, I really wished they would have told me privately. I worried that I might freak out in front of all my friends. When Dr. Grist came out he spoke to us briefly and then told me that he and I needed to be c wn at a press conference in a few minutes.

This is where I really appreciated Indy and Vicki and Suzanne because everyone wanted to hug me and tell me how grateful they were that the surgery went well. I was relieved and happy too, but I needed to get going and my emotions were on edge. My three friends whisked me outside and the four of us just sat and cried until it was time for me to go to the press conference.

As I sat at a table with Dr. Grist and looked into the camera lights, I prayed I would not pass out. I'm not good in those situations and didn't know how I would act or what I would say. Then I noticed Lowery, "Dr. Gobinson," standing in the back, still in his scrubs. My legs were shaking so bad I just hoped I wouldn't embarrass my husband and pass out on national television.

Fortunately, the press conference was short, and we were then rushed out of the room. Dr. Bob said, "Follow me to the recovery room."

Brett lay there, still, his eyes closed. I sat on a high stool next to him and leaned over to stare into his face. He began to stir. Bob said, "He's doing very well. He's going to seem like he's awake, but he won't be. You'll need to keep talking to him, and don't be surprised if you have to repeat yourself several times. He'll keep asking you the same questions. Just keep answering him."

A nurse came over to check his monitor. She pulled back the covers. Brett opened his eyes and pulled the covers back up. "She's been trying to peek at me all day," he said.

I laughed and shot a glance at Bob. "Eveline," he said, "you just can't imagine the things he might say."

Brett said hi to me.

I said, "Hi, honey. Everything went well. The surgery's over."

Brett asked me how everything went, whether he had already had the surgery, if he was all right—over and over and over. I kept assuring him everything was fine.

The nurse came back to check on something and Brett said, "She's peeking at me again. She wants to get a look."

I apologized to her. She said, "Oh, don't worry. He'll say a lot of things. I get this all the time."

After about twenty or thirty minutes of answering the same questions over and over, I thought he should finally be coming out of it. He leaned over and tried to grab me amorously. I pushed his hands away. "Would you cut it out? This is not the time or place!"

"Oh, come on. Come on, honey."

"Brett Butler, you are in a hospital!"

Brett said, "You can tell Walt that prayer meeting didn't work! I was in there sweating my butt off, and for what?"

Gradually it registered with him that he was out of surgery and, for the most part, he was fine. They began preparing the bed to wheel him back up to his room. The nurse came to unhook the heart monitors and take off the sticky patch from his chest. She gave it a quick pull, and he opened his eyes. "You tell her if she does that again I'm going to hit her!"

I said, "He won't hit you. I promise."

As they wheeled him out and down the hall, he was yelling, "Wheee! Whoaa!" He yelled all the way down the hall, talking and blabbing and babbling. By the time we got back to the room, he was exhausted again. He lay still with his eyes shut as they eased him through the doorway.

Most of the big crowd had left by then, but several of our closest friends were still there. They fell silent and serious as Brett was rolled into the room. They looked him over carefully as he lay still, his eyes shut. Suddenly he said, "Will you all quit staring at me?"

Everybody burst out laughing. Brett told me later that he remembered virtually nothing from the time I left him before surgery and the time they wheeled him back into the room. The last thing he remembered before having to let go of my hand was that everyone looked so worried and concerned. Several hours later, finally coming out of it, he had a feeling he was back in the same place, and they were still looking at him.

Bobby Harju showed up that afternoon and stayed with Ben and Beverly and me in that beautiful suite of rooms. It was such a homey, domestic atmosphere, that it really helped us provide hospitality to all the people who came to see Brett.

Maybe other people wouldn't want that much company while they're trying to recuperate from surgery, but I felt warmed by all the attention. It was good that so many friends from Atlanta could be there, and Bobby Harju came from Chicago. A few days later, my college coach Doc Parham and his wife showed up. They were traveling and decided to drive all the way over to Atlanta when they heard I was going in for surgery. Most of that time is a blur in my memory. I remember sleeping a lot, waking up, cracking a few jokes, and falling back to sleep. I tried to stay upbeat.

I was asleep when Doc finally had to leave, and when I woke up a letter was waiting for me from him. Bobby Harju recalls: "We'd all been holding up fairly well with our friend in such deep trouble. Then Brett started to read that letter, and you could hear a pin drop. Tears were just pouring down our faces. Brett looked up and it was amazing. He never choked up while reading it. He just said, 'That's really, really nice.' He sat there for a second and said, 'I've got to lie down. I'm tired.'

"We had gone several days without breaking down, but that letter really did it to us."

One of the hardest things for Eveline, I know, was when my bandages were changed. She had been told how long the incisions would be, but I don't think anything prepares you for what your husband will look like with thirty-two staples in his neck. At first she didn't want the kids to see me until I got home, but Mary, our nanny, convinced her they really needed to do so.

When they first came in the room, they held back, looking at my neck. I told them, "Come on kids, I'm fine. Come sit on my lap." They climbed up into the bed with me. I hope it gave them a sense of security and peace. It was wonderful to have them there.

Jay Howell, a friend of ours who pitched for the Dodgers and lives in Atlanta, came to see me. He said, "Hey, Brett, all you need is two bolts right here in your neck, and you'd look just like Frankenstein."

Fifty lymph nodes were removed during surgery and the news from the tests was almost as good as we hoped. Only one had cancerous tissue. Obviously, it would have been preferable if none of them had. I went home to recuperate and get ready for radiation treatments, which were scheduled to begin about a month later. Eveline sat out on the veranda for hours and read the thousands and thousands of letters that poured in. She said sitting there and crying was the best therapy she could have.

She told me, "Those letters not only gave me an opportunity to cry and get all my emotions out, but it also allowed me to realize that the public doesn't view you as just a baseball player. They really do understand what a wonderful man you are on and off the field. You have invested in the lives of people, including thousands you've never even met."

A little more than a week after surgery, I announced that I would try to return to the Dodgers during the 1996 season, even if it was just as a spectator. Of course, I wanted to come back as a center fielder. I didn't just want to be there for team morale. I wanted to contribute. That became my passion, my goal. To everybody (including Eveline) but me, that goal seemed ludicrous. Maybe it was, but it kept me going.

Eveline became a superstar in nutrition and medical research. Just before my birthday in June, we were driving to church and my sister, Bev, was with us. Eveline was racking her brain, trying to think of ways to build up my immune system. She remembered that reactivating the thymus helped some people's immune systems produce T cells to fight infection. All of a sudden, she said, "Oh my gosh. That article. Where is that article?"

"What are you talking about?" Beverly said.

Eveline said, "A man gave Brett an article last January about a vitamin supplement that helps people. I've got to find that article."

After church, Eveline tore our house apart and finally found the article that man had given me after my speaking engagement six months earlier. She went to our chiropractor, Pam Putnam, who became our link to information. She found all kinds of supplements for me to take, things that would get the radiation out of my body quickly after the treatments I would have to take soon. Pam also located the doctor who wrote that paper, tracking him down in Savannah. He told her, "This is amazing, because we've been using that supplement for the last two years only in studies. Tomorrow we make it available to the public for the first time."

She told him to send her a case of it right away. We're convinced it made a huge difference in my recovery. Between Pam and Mackie Shilstone, we got all kinds of nutrients and supplements that gave me every chance to heal quickly.

When the Mets were in town to play Atlanta, five of them came to see me: Rico Brogna, Doug Henry, Jerry DiPoto, Blas Minor, and Bobby Jones. I had been particularly close to those guys in our Bible studies and many discussions. Though I was only in New York for four months and played only ninety games, we had really bonded. It was very encouraging to see them.

John Cunningham, whose son attended school with Blake, had been battling cancer with the help of American Biologics in Tijuana, Mexico. He was urging me to check them out and to at least use a combination of alternative and traditional medicine. That resonated with Eveline, who was sure that chemotherapy was not the way to go and that radiation treatment, by itself, could do as much harm as good. So we flew to California and then visited Tijuana to check out American Biologics.

While in California, I decided to drop in on my teammates at Dodger Stadium. They were stunned to see me and encouraged that I looked so good. My scar was still bright red, but having not begun radiation yet, otherwise I looked fairly normal. I told them I was eager to get back and join them, and I felt they were mostly being polite when they encouraged me. I heard that when the team was on the road, they set up my locker with my uniform and equipment as if they were waiting for me to join them at any moment. I was touched.

That night I watched the game against the Cincinnati Reds from Fred Claire's box. I didn't know they were going to mention on the P.A. system that I was there, so it was an incredible thrill to get a big ovation and be able to wave to the fans from up there. Most gratifying to me was that the Reds came out of their dugout to acknowledge me as well.

On my birthday, June 15, Eveline threw a huge party at the house because the Dodgers were in town. What a day that was. They all got limos and came out for a big barbecue. I was feeling pretty good by then, but I knew tough times were ahead. Two days later, I would begin radiation treatments that would last for six weeks.

We had gone through a lot of soul-searching and debate about what to do. I wanted to try a combination of the radiation and building up my immune system. But I had to decide if I was going to go to American Biologics in Tijuana while doing my radiation nearby in Chula Vista, California. I was thinking I would do three weeks of radiation in Chula Vista while going to American Biologics each day, and then I'd come back and do the rest in Atlanta. I was advised to do it all in one place, so I decided to pray about it.

The night before I had to make a decision it seemed I woke up every hour on the hour. I kept praying, *Lord, I have to make a choice.* I finally got up and went into the den and fell on my face and said, *Lord, I don't even know how to pray. Let your Spirit go before me and pray for me, because I need to know by tomorrow what I'm going to do.*

The next day I got a call from my radiologist. He said, "Brett, I have a clear feeling that you need to do it all here in Atlanta." That was my answer.

The first radiation treatment was painless, but the most difficult. I had to sit still for an hour and a half while they measured me and marked me. In the future they would use those markings and zap me quickly. My daughter Stefanie was a little trouper. She went with me for almost every radiation treatment. She watched as they put me in a chamber, masked my face, clamped me down, and shot the radiation into my neck.

We had decided in advance that I was not going to let the

radiation affect my immune system and then lose a bunch of weight before starting to build back up. Between Pam and Mackie and Eveline finding stuff for me to take and things for me to drink, I was on a pretty serious regimen to keep my strength up.

I had been told I would be able to eat normally until about three weeks into radiation, when it would be impossible for me to keep anything down. Probably because of all the supplements and nutrients I was taking, I was still eating regular food into the sixth week. My weight had stayed the same, but during that sixth week I developed a couple of dozen sores in my mouth. I had to try to numb them with medicine so I could eat. Soon, chewing and swallowing became a chore.

I had also been told that though the radiation treatments took just a few minutes each day, they would build and build and build on each other. By the second week I would begin to feel a little nauseated. The third week was supposed to bring on a sore throat from the radiation burning the tissue. The fourth week it was supposed to really hurt. The fifth week I was going to wish I was dead, and the sixth week I was going to survive only by knowing it was the last week. I was also supposed to lose a bunch of weight.

But I made it all the way to the sixth week, still eating solid food and maintaining my weight. We started to wonder if maybe the radiation wasn't being done correctly because I had so few symptoms. I was encouraged, except for those sores in my mouth. That sixth week, though, I finally began to lose weight, and lose it rapidly.

The last day of my radiation treatments was July 29, 1996. We flew into L.A., and before heading down to American Biologics, I went to see the Dodgers again. In the six weeks since they had last seen me, I had nearly wasted away. I weighed less than 150 pounds, my throat was sore and raspy, and I looked like death warmed over. I could see the pity in their eyes. They couldn't believe how quickly I had deteriorated. For whatever encouragement there might have been from my earlier trip, these guys now believed they were looking into the face of death.

I kept trying to encourage them and said that I was going to be fine, that I was still fighting my way back. They nodded and pretended to agree, but it was clear no one thought I was ever going to play baseball again.

Following my intravenous injections in Tijuana, we came back to a hotel near the L.A. airport, because we were leaving early the next morning to fly back to Atlanta. Eveline was trying to get me to eat. I couldn't think of anything that sounded good. Finally she gave me some ice cream. Boy, did that feel good going down. But suddenly I felt excruciating pain. I ran into the bathroom and spit into the sink. There was blood everywhere. I screamed for Eveline and told her to call 911. Instead she called the Dodger trainers, who urged her to rush me to Cedars Sinai.

I was scared to death. Our cab driver took us to the wrong medical center, and by the time we got to the right one, Eveline and I were both panicky.

My plan had been to go back to Atlanta and then head to New Orleans to work personally with Mackie Shilstone on building myself up and getting back with the Dodgers before the end of the season. Now, as they checked me into the hospital, I had no idea what would happen to those plans.

THE
COMEBACK

What had happened to me was not as bad as it sounded. It was scary, and it was gross, and we wouldn't want to have to go through it again, but the explanation was fairly simple. The doctor at Cedars Sinai told me that the radiation treatments had, naturally, wreaked havoc on the tissue in my throat. Now that I was healing, I had actually developed scabs there. Swallowing food tore those scabs off and caused bleeding. The recommendation from the doctors? Even more gross. I was to go ahead and eat and let it happen. And I was to swallow all that residue and blood. It sounds awful, but I had to eat.

Peter O'Malley had given me a little gadget called Sports Trax, a beeper-sized monitor that allowed me to keep up with the Dodgers. Scores of their games would appear on the LED readout just like phone numbers appear on a beeper. I had the feeling I was still a Dodger, that they were still waiting for me, and that I would eventually make it back. I didn't want to be a mascot, an inspiration, a morale booster. I wanted to be the starting center fielder and leadoff man.

I wouldn't realize it until later, but I was the only person in the world who really believed I could do it.

Eveline was my biggest supporter from the beginning, of course. But she also remembered when a little piece of pasta took me fifteen minutes to eat. I'd push my plate away, but she'd make me eat. Watching me struggle like that made her realize how tough it was for me and how unlikely it would be that I could ever rebuild my strength in time to rejoin the Dodgers in 1996.

Doc Parham visited me in the hospital after my second surgery. He recalls: "Brett looked awful. It just broke my heart. He could hardly swallow, and he could hardly talk. He was already talking that day about coming back, but I think he was just talking, and we were all hoping."

I was sick, wasted, exhausted. And yet I couldn't wait to get to Atlanta and then on to New Orleans where I planned to work with Mackie Shilstone. He's like a brother to me. I've known him since I was in San Francisco and he was hired by the Giants. I've visited him every year since then in New Orleans. He prescribes my diet, my nutrients, my supplements, and he works me out.

As you can imagine, I didn't feel much like eating anything after that incident with the ice cream and the trip to Cedars Sinai. I was afraid I would be tempted to cough up the food and the scabs, which is where all the bleeding would come from. The idea of just swallowing everything made me as nauseated as it must make you to read this. But Eveline kept pushing me to eat.

She recalls: "I kept telling him, 'You've got to eat something.' I was thinking, *He's getting skinnier and skinnier.*

"The day after we got home from L.A., we left for New Orleans. Bart Wiley, Walt's son (our publicist), came along to help me with the media and the kids. We would keep them busy for a couple of weeks until they had to go back to Atlanta for school. Meanwhile Brett would be in intensive therapy and training with Mackie. I'll never forget sitting on the plane to New Orleans and looking over at my sleeping husband and thinking, *What are we doing? He can't do this. He physically can't do this.*"

Mackie Shilstone is an energetic, enthusiastic, optimistic guy, but he didn't think I could do it either. I could see it in his eyes, and later he told me his first thought on seeing me was, *There's no way.* I was checked out thoroughly by the Kenner Center doctors, and I kept telling Mackie, "We're gonna do this."

He said, "Yeah, we'll do it!" But it was hard for him to maintain eye contact when he said it. I couldn't blame him.

The Brett Morgan Butler who looked back at me from the mirror every day looked hollow and lifeless. I wanted that old gleam in the eye, that sharpness to the expression, that determined, confident look. I didn't want to pause and think long enough to realize what a crazy thing I was doing. It seemed I had already been through hell, and now I wanted to get back to the Dodgers within three weeks. It was ludicrous, but I was focused and determined. My whole life had been full of obstacles, challenges, roadblocks, people telling me I was too this or too that. I was not about to admit I had met my match now. With God's help, I was going to get this thing done.

Every night and every morning Eveline made me milkshakes with all the stuff in them I needed to help my body recuperate from the workouts and continue to heal and build up. I would leave every morning, work out with Mackie all day, and get back around five o'clock. Every day it was the same thing, a sort of mini-spring training.

Mackie had put together a medical team of neurologists, internists, oncologists, and orthopedists. I ate in the hospital cafeteria under his guidance. Mackie even arranged it so I could work out with the New Orleans Zephyrs, a Brewers Class AAA farm club.

Each morning I started in the sports performance center, lifting weights. Then Mackie put me through a series of exercises for my upper body. This was full-time work, and I was committed to it. I felt myself getting stronger, though I may not have looked it at first. When it came time for Eveline and Bart to take the kids back to Atlanta for school, it was already late August. I didn't have much time. My goal was not to make it back to the big leagues by 1997. I wanted it now.

Eveline remembers: "Though Brett was getting stronger and doing better, when I left him I thought, *He can't play. He just can't.* A week later, when I went to pick him up at the airport, I couldn't believe it. I was stunned. When he walked off that plane, it was like the old Brett. Except for that scar on his neck, it was as if nothing had happened to him. He was strong. He was muscular. He looked great. His color was better. Most striking of all, he had gained eighteen pounds in nineteen days. I said, 'Brett, I can't believe the transformation. It literally is a miracle.' "

The last time I had seen the Dodgers I had been ravaged by radiation treatments and my inability to eat much. For an athlete who never topped out at much more than 160 pounds to start with, losing more than ten percent of his body weight makes a huge difference. Most of my teammates, if they're honest, will admit they didn't give me one chance in ten of ever playing big-league baseball again. Most of them, I think, wondered if I would survive at all. Had I been an impartial observer, I don't know what kind of chance I would have given myself.

I called the Dodgers to tell them I wanted to join them on the road in Montreal. Frankly, the reception I got made it clear they would be happy to have me come and watch the games. I wanted to do more than watch. Maybe I wasn't ready to play right away, but I wanted to suit up, to work out with the team, to take batting practice, to throw the ball around. I wanted to sit on that bench as a Dodger who could be used in a pinch. And when they returned to Los Angeles on September 6 to play the Pirates, my goal was to be in the lineup. I told them that Mackie and the trainers and the doctors had all cleared me. I said, "I'm coming back to play."

"Sure, Brett," Bill Russell said, "whatever you say. If you want to meet us in Montreal, come on up."

Under my street clothes, I wore a sleeveless shirt that read: "It's not how good you are, it's how bad you want it." Nothing could have more perfectly represented my outlook. I carried a water bottle everywhere I went, my saliva glands having been rendered useless.

Though my teammates were stunned to see that I had gained weight and muscle mass, and most of them said things like, "Oh, Bugsy, it's nice to have you back," I don't think anybody there actually thought I could play. It had not been that long ago that they had seen just how sick I looked.

When I got in the cage to take batting practice, hitting coach Reggie Smith said, "Okay, let's take a couple of cuts. Be careful."

It was all I could do to keep from grinning. I was back where I belonged, and I wasn't about to be careful like a weak little old man who could barely walk. After laying down a few bunts, I started driving balls to the outfield. *Whack! Whack! Whack!*

Reggie was surprised. After about fifty swings I walked past the third-base dugout and smiled at the guys. "Did I convince you?" They sat there shaking their heads in amazement. I ran the bases, took some fly balls, and ran wind sprints. I told everybody I wanted to be in the lineup when the Dodgers returned to Los Angeles September 6.

On Thursday, August 29, Bill Russell had me stand in against Darren Hall, who was coming back from elbow surgery. It provided the Dodgers a good look at both of us. I hit the ball well. Darren said later he didn't have the heart to come too far inside on me. That wouldn't have bothered me.

I won't lie to you; I was certainly not back in top form yet. I was feeling my age, not to mention my disease and all the medication that went with it. This was work, more work than it had ever been before, but there was nothing I would have rather done.

It had been fourteen weeks since I had left the club for what I thought was a tonsillectomy. Word began getting around in Los Angeles that I would make my comeback on September 6.

Eveline flew out. My sister and brother and my best friend, Dave Hinman, and his wife, Terry, came. So did Dr. Bob and Kathy Gadlage.

They all had a great time, and I was run a little ragged making several media appearances. The day before the first game of the series against Montreal, I was on *The Tonight Show with Jay Leno.*

I was so excited I could hardly sleep. I wasn't going to be a sub. I was going to start and play center field, right where I belonged.

Eveline remembers: "To be perfectly honest, I thought his comeback had been awfully quick. But I also figured, nobody's going to stop him. He's doing what he wants to do. He has nothing to prove. He beat cancer. Playing in this game is nothing. I got caught up in the moment of it. I convinced myself he was back, he was playing baseball, and everything would be the way it once was."

It was appropriate that we played the Mets on the road before coming back to Los Angeles. That had given Eveline and me a chance to see some of the friends we had made when I played those ninety games with the Mets. And that was when, after four months of being the strong one, Eveline began to cry. Every time she thought about what I had been through, how badly I had wanted to return, and how hard I had worked for this, she had to wipe away tears. She told sportswriter Tim Brown, who had become our friend, "It's an ending and a new beginning. God's got us through it. It's closure. I'll probably sit there in L.A. and cry the whole time. It's bizarre to think it's actually happening. I always believed it would, but now it's here. And I want so badly for him to be happy with how it's all ended. God has blessed us so much. I almost feel like it's undeserved. I've been thinking about his mom a lot now. I'm sure he's thinking about her not being here."

My brother, Ben, told Tim, "For me, this symbolizes what Brett's inner drive is. That anything is possible. I think he had this planned all along. No matter what it took, he was going to be out there."

It wasn't unusual to have a big crowd at a Friday night game in September when the Dodgers were in the thick of a pennant race. On September 6 more than 41,000 fans were jammed in the stadium. I was so excited I could have wet my pants. When I stepped onto the field, long before the game would begin, and simply began to do my stretching exercises, I received a huge ovation. That put a lump in my throat that wouldn't go away until after my first at bat.

As I went through my usual pre-game rituals, I thought of the duffel bag in my locker that carried the containers for the seventy pills I swallowed every twenty-four hours. I thought of the fact that I was taking Laetrile intravenously three times a week. I realized that after the game I would be on an I.V. for twenty minutes.

The whole experience, the excitement, the nervousness, the eagerness to get out there, reminded me of the first time I put on a baseball uniform when I was six years old. I also remembered the excitement of my first major-league game in August of 1981. Throughout batting practice, loosening up, and running wind sprints, I accepted encouragement from everybody I saw.

Foremost in my mind was that as important as this comeback was to me, I had a job to do. We needed to win to get back into first place, and the last thing I wanted was that my comeback would somehow get in the way of that. It may have been enough for everybody else that I simply returned to the game, even if I went 0-4 and made an error or two, but that's not what I was there for. I wanted to focus on not just coming back, but on getting on base, stealing a base, scoring a run, doing whatever I had to do to help this team win.

When they announced the starting lineups, a roar thundered from the stands. I felt the eyes of my teammates on me in the dugout, and I couldn't wait to run out to center field for the top of the first inning. Finally, it was time to go. As I ran onto the field, the crowd erupted again. After we set down the Pirates, the moment of truth came.

I knew I would be welcomed to the plate to lead off the bottom of the first, but nothing can prepare you for how you'll feel when more than 41,000 people rise *en masse* to cheer the announcement of your name. My hands were cold and clammy, my knees were knocking. I touched the bill of my helmet as I walked toward the batter's box. The sound was deafening.

As I prepared to step in, sobs rose in my throat. I couldn't get my composure. Though the catcher squatted there, the umpire stood back and the pitcher, Francisco Cordova, stood away from the rubber. This half inning was not going to begin until that huge crowd decided it would. I stepped out and held my batting helmet aloft. The crowd went crazy. I felt my eyes filling. For nearly a minute, the cheers rained down on me. The people were welcoming me, congratulating me, wishing me the best, loving me. I knew if I didn't step into the batter's box right away, I would be worthless.

I prayed Cordova would start me with a fastball. I was in no condition to start thinking about working the count, reading the defense, and all that. I turned on that first pitch, a fastball, and grounded out to second base.

I got pretty much the same reaction in the third inning, and had to acknowledge the crowd once again. My teammates began kidding me, "We're trying to play a baseball game here, if you don't mind."

During that at bat, I had the presence of mind to take a couple of pitches. Then I tried to steer the ball and flew out to left field.

Reggie Smith pulled me aside when I came in. "Man, just try to hit it," he said.

By the fifth inning and my third at bat I felt like myself again. I worked the count to 2-2 before hitting a single to left. I stood at first, enjoying the cheers for something I had done in the game, not just because I was making a comeback.

In the eighth I worked the count full and then drew a walk. The pitcher kept trying to pick me off first, knowing I probably wanted to steal. When I did go, I was so slow and had such a bad jump that a good throw would have had me by ten feet. But the throw bounced into center field and I kept going. Eric Karros sacrificed me in from third and I slid in with what proved to be the winning run. That was my idea of a comeback. Not just to show up, but to contribute. That game meant more to me than any other in my life.

I was replaced, exhausted, in the ninth inning. But I started the next night and went 2-4 in a one-run victory over the Pirates. The next day I was 0-2 but had two walks, and somebody asked me if I needed a day off. I said, "My goal is to play every day."

I was busier than I had ever been. Everybody wanted me on talk shows. I did a lot of them, but my plan was to slow down and conserve my energy. In the back of my mind was a nagging memory of my dear friend Dave Dravecky, who broke his arm five days after his triumphant return.

Eveline came to our Tuesday night game, five days after my first game back, and was going to watch us play Cincinnati before leaving the next day.

Frankly, I was worried about what was going on in my body. The past five days had been hard work and the most stressful of my life. My lips were blistered, and Eveline worried that my immune system might be getting depleted because of the stress. There may have even been a recurrence of the cancer. We just didn't know.

God has always had a way of getting my attention and forcing me to slow down when necessary. In the fourth inning I was trying to get a bunt down off Reds right-hander Giovanni Carrara. I squared around on the kid, and I thought he had thrown the ball outside. I decided to go out and get it and push it down the third base line. But the pitch ran in on me and I couldn't pull back in time to keep from being hit on the pinkie. I went down in a heap.

Eveline remembers: "All the hoopla was done. Everybody was gone. Our friends had left. I was sitting with other Dodger wives when Brett went down. The exact thing had happened to him in Cleveland on opening day of 1986. It was *déjà vu*. I knew his hand was broken. Immediately I left my seat and started walking up the steps. Eric Karros's parents looked sympathetically at me. I put my hand on Eric's father's shoulder as I passed and said, 'George, I'm going to get my husband, and I'm taking him home.'

"George Karros said, 'Bless your heart.' "

Eveline rode along with me on the way to the emergency room. I was pretty sure the finger was broken, but I kept trying to tell her, and myself, that maybe it wasn't. She said, "Of course it's broken, what else can it be?"

In the emergency room they called in a specialist to maneuver the bones back into place. They tried to numb the area with an injection, which really hurt. I yelped and then moaned as he worked the bones. That's when Eveline lost it. As soon as that doctor was out of the room, she burst into tears. "I can't take this anymore," she said. "I don't understand. Why would God bring us all this way and now let this happen? I don't see the purpose."

I said, "Honey, it's okay. I really feel God is saying to me that I've done everything he wanted me to do. Now it's time to rest." For some reason, knowing the bone was broken and would have to be in a cast was a relief to me.

Eveline recalls: "In the end I came to realize that the added breaking of his hand was just more of a testimony to the Lord. Brett could have freaked out like I did. Rather than telling the media that this was just God's way of telling him to take a break and get his full strength back, he could have given up. If anybody ever had a right to, he did—after having been let go by the Dodgers, coming back and going through the replacement player fiasco, his mom dying of cancer, his grandmother dying, his getting cancer, and then breaking his hand. I mean, anyone would have forgiven him if he had wanted to cash it all in. But he didn't make excuses. He saw this as another challenge."

I honestly believed I was going to come back and help the

Dodgers. I foresaw them making the World Series and me contributing to winning the pennant. Then I was going to retire. That's what I really thought would happen. Lowery Robinson had a dream about that. He said, "If you guys get there and you do that, I'm gonna say I knew it would happen."

When the Dodgers didn't make it, I had to resign myself to the fact that the purpose of that broken finger was to get me to rest.

I stayed with the team and took the cast off earlier than I should have. I was really working that hand, hoping to come back. Eveline saw me swinging a bat outside the Dodgers dugout during a series in Atlanta and hollered at me from the stands, "Shame on you! Put that down!"

The joke around our house during the off-season was that one day I was "definitely" going to play, the next I was going to retire "for sure." I told Fred Claire that I would probably retire. He told me not to make any rash decisions, that it was too early. Every time I brought it up at home, Bart or Eveline would laugh and say, "Just let us know the day before spring training whether you're going or not." It seemed every day I came down on a different side of the decision.

Worse, though, was that I began losing weight again. I got down to about 145 pounds and was worried that I would not be able to get a handle on my health. I didn't want to quit baseball, not like this. I wanted to go out on my own terms. Not many people get to do that.

Suddenly, I was not a fun guy to live with.

TWENTY-ONE

ONE MORE BLOW

You'd think a guy who had been through what I've been through and learned the lessons I've learned would be so grateful and so humble before God that he would become a model Christian. Sorry. I'm still human. I still have a sin nature.

Being unable to snap back quickly from the hand injury the way I had from the cancer put me on edge. I was still getting Laetrile injections and taking lots of vitamins, but I was dehydrated and underweight. I tried to keep the family out of it. I wanted to put a distance between me and them and deal with this on my own.

One day I had an argument with Abbi, our oldest teenager. I had told her to do something several times, and when I discovered it still wasn't done, I blew up. It didn't make any difference to me that she had a friend over and that they were playing a game. I rushed in there, told her off, and flipped that game all over the room.

Her friend sat there amazed and embarrassed. Abbi screamed

and ran to her room. Eveline said, "Brett! What is the matter with you?"

I didn't want to hear it. I had enough troubles of my own. My veins were collapsing and it was hard to get the Laetrile injections to work. I was miserable. I thought I had an excuse to be short-tempered. Maybe I did, but the family suffered.

I went shopping with Eveline and found myself grumpy even about her choice of clothes for the girls. The clerk was complimenting her selection when I snapped, "That's not a pretty dress. That's an ugly dress. That'll make her look poverty-stricken."

Eveline told me to just go busy myself elsewhere and keep out of it. She was afraid I would make a scene in public.

Later, when we were having lunch, I was given the wrong dressing on my salad. Normally I take pride in being very friendly with waiters and waitresses, even if they forget something or do something wrong. Now, however, I was mad. "Can't you just get it right?"

The young man took my salad away to fix it, and as he was leaving I said, "That's why you're working in a job like this."

Eveline really let me have it. "Brett Butler, what is wrong with you? Who exactly are you angry at? Me? The kids? God? We didn't give you cancer. We don't deserve to have you take it out on us. You're throwing stuff around the house, you're screaming at your daughter, you're yelling at me. You're treating people rudely."

"I wasn't rude."

"Yes, you were. You need to re-evaluate your attitude. If you're angry at God, talk to him about it. We don't need this. We've all had enough stress in our lives. You've come through and you've done great and you've made your comeback. Okay, you broke your hand. So what? Big deal. You think no one is worse off than you? What about our friends from church with the sick daughter? Your kids are healthy. You'd better start looking at the positive things in your life and all the good things that are going on rather than just sitting there saying, 'Oh poor me!' "

Eveline was right, of course, but it wasn't working. I was not in the mood. I said, "I don't need to hear this."

"Yeah, you do. You may not want to listen, but you need to hear it. Brett, you've changed. You used to be positive. You used to be kind and loving to everyone. You've become a negative, mean person. I don't even know who you are anymore."

Of course that made me mad. Our meal evolved into an awkward silence. Later, I went to pick up Abbi from cheerleading practice. When she got in the car she said, "Dad, can I say something to you?"

I said, "Yeah, sure."

"You know, Daddy, ever since you got cancer, you've changed. You used to be so nice. But now lots of times you're not anymore."

I was so stunned to hear Abbi say the same thing her mother had just told me, I couldn't even respond. I fought tears the whole way home.

Later I went to the hospital for my Laetrile injections. A nurse there told me a lot of the troubles in her life, and suddenly I realized Eveline was right. I was not the only one going through tough times.

As soon as I got in the car to go home, I began crying. It was only a five-minute drive, but I cried the whole way home.

When I walked in, my eyes were red. Eveline followed me into the back room. She said, "Are you all right?"

Abbi saw me and followed me too. I said, "Get the other kids and let's go into the kitchen."

The kids were talking among themselves, saying, "Dad's crying."

When the six of us were together in the kitchen, I asked them to kneel with me. I apologized. "I need you to forgive me for being such a jerk. I've been trying to handle this thing on my own, and I haven't done a good job with it. I've taken it out on you, and you don't deserve it."

Soon we were all crying. Abbi looked up at me and said, "Dad, it's nice to see you cry."

"Why?"

"Because it makes me realize I don't have to be perfect."

That was a major point of healing and turnaround for me and for the family. Eveline says I was still a hypochondriac, though. I was bothered by and complained about every tiny ailment in my body. She said if I had a hangnail, I worried it was going to kill me.

Eveline recalls: "We had gone somewhere to eat with the kids. Brett was going on and on about something hurting on this side and something feeling strange over here and worrying about this and worrying about that. I had had enough. Finally I lost it. I said, 'You know what, Brett? It's cancer, and you're gonna die. That's it. You're just gonna die.'

"The kids stared at me as if they couldn't believe I would say that. Brett and I just looked at each other and began laughing. I said, 'Brett, you're a hypochondriac! You've got terminal hypochondria. It's not cancer, and you're not gonna die!'"

That was just what I needed.

At the beginning of 1997, I was still undecided about my future. I was getting stronger, feeling better, getting myself built back up, but again, every other day I decided I'd had enough. I would retire. The next day? Maybe I'll try it.

Eveline and I went out to California for the American Music Awards, and while I was there I stopped in at Dodger Stadium to watch the first winter workout. Eric Karros was having a press conference, announcing his new deal with the Dodgers, and I began getting the bug again.

Fred Claire asked me what I was going to do, and I told him I really didn't know. He urged me not to make a decision until after spring training. Before I knew it, word got out that I was going to take another shot at baseball.

One thing I was not going to do: I was not going to experiment in spring training. If I packed my bags and flew to Vero Beach, I was going down there to earn my spot on this team. I wanted to be center fielder and lead-off man for the Dodgers on opening day. Anything less would be a failure, and I would rather retire.

When it became apparent that I was still able to produce and that I was going to reach my goal, I announced I would play in the 1997 season. But I made it clear that this was my last year. I believed the Dodgers had a shot at the World Series in 1997, and I wanted to be a part of it. People asked me, "What if you hit .360 and are named MVP?"

I knew how unlikely that was, considering I would turn forty in June, but I reiterated, "I'm done after this. I'm going home to spend time with my family. My kids are still young."

I was the first Dodger hitter to come to the plate on opening day against the Phillies. Again I had to step out to acknowledge a standing ovation. I wondered how long it would be before L.A. fans got tired of continually welcoming back the comeback kid. The Dodgers started quickly, and it was fun to be on a winning team. I was hitting fairly well, flirting with .300 for a couple of weeks. Then, as if on a silver platter, I was given one of those career games.

In just five weeks I would celebrate the one-year anniversary of my cancer surgery and reach a major milestone of remaining clear of the disease. Against the Mets in Shea Stadium, on April 16, I went 5-for-5 and raised my batting average to .311 and my on-base percentage to .446, tops in the National League for lead-off hitters.

I told reporters, "I didn't have a fear of failure, but I wasn't sure I could do this. I don't think I'll ever think I'm totally back. I'll always have this reminder, this numbness in my neck."

It was the fifth five-hit game in my career, and the first time I had done that since April of 1994, which also happened in New York.

Just over two weeks later, on May 4, I threw out the Florida Marlins Bobby Bonilla at the plate from center field and felt something tear in my shoulder. I was convinced I had just strained it, but it didn't get better despite my sitting out for six days. An MRI revealed what team doctor Frank Jobe said was a "superior labrum tear of the shoulder."

Dr. Jobe said, "It's a fairly large tear. It didn't look entirely new. It could have been there a long time, but the throw made it worse." I was immediately placed on the disabled list for fifteen days, but Jobe predicted I would be out a minimum of four weeks. He also said the tear would be unlikely to heal without surgery.

Three days later, knowing it might be my last appearance, I pinch hit in the seventh inning and received another great ovation from the fans. I fouled off eight pitches before popping out to the shortstop in shallow left field. That left me hitting .356, but that was little consolation. It was hard to believe I was out again.

When I began this book I wrote that unless something happened, I was the oldest lead-off man and center fielder in the majors. Well, you see what happened. If the shoulder requires surgery, it's unlikely I would come back in time to help the Dodgers even in the postseason. That will be my goal, of course, but if it doesn't happen, that will mean I left the game other than by my own terms. It would have been great to finish the season and win a World Series and then voluntarily retire. Regardless, I'm not changing my mind. I've promised my family, and I'm at peace with the decision. No matter what happens, I won't be playing baseball in 1998.

My dream, my desire, my goal was to play again this year. God allowed that to happen, and I am thankful for one last season—however long it lasts, however it ends. I put on the uniform and was able to do what I've done best since I was six years old.

I've learned so much in the last two years. Life is not about circumstances. Life is about attitude. God allowed me to step back and see how blessed I am, much like the story of George Bailey in

It's A Wonderful Life. That was a rare and interesting privilege. I've come to realize that through having cancer my life was blessed and enriched. God gave me nothing I wanted, but everything I needed.

Hope is in all of us. The ability to overcome any situation comes when we refuse to accept the impossible and make it possible.

I have no control over my life. Ultimately God does. The bottom line is that my future is in his hands. That's true of everybody and it's the reason I wanted to tell this story. God is in control. He knows best. Everything that happens to us happens for a reason. Our job is to determine that reason and make sure God gets the glory.

APPENDIX I

A sampling of the 180,000 letters Brett & Eveline received from well-wishers

Dear Eveline:

You and Brett have been so heavy on my heart. I love you both and I continue to pray for Brett as he undergoes radiation. I'm especially praying for you, Eveline, because I know this is such a demanding time for you physically and emotionally.

Looking forward to hearing all the things the Father is showing you during this difficult time—I know I will be the richer after hearing it! Learning to trust God in adversity can be such a slow and difficult process—but the fruit is so awesome.

Love, Jackie Kendall

(*author of* Lunatic on a Limb for Jesus)

Mr. Butler:

On a summer evening in 1983, I attended my first major-league baseball game in Atlanta. My favorite player was Dale Murphy because of his wholesome image. That was until a young, determined outfielder by the name of Brett Butler came to the plate in a crucial situation in a late-inning game. He got what turned out to be the game winner for the Braves. From then on I had two heroes on the team. What made me notice him immediately was his size. I had assumed wrongly that you had to be big to make it in professional sports. I told myself if someone Brett's size can make it, maybe I can too.

My dreams of becoming a major-leaguer never panned out. That's okay, though. A young boy can always live out his dreams through the accomplishments of his hero.

Fast forward to August 18, 1993, to that same ball park in Atlanta. Now, along with my hero, I am wearing Dodger blue. It was on this evening that I finally got your John Hancock on an old baseball card. I was too nervous and excited to say anything then. I regret that now. That card is still framed and sitting beside my bed.

Earlier today, I found out the hard way what makes a person a hero. ESPN told me today you are now battling throat cancer. You've always come off as a fighter. I urge you to fight this until you are cured. I want you to know your fans will stick by you through this ordeal. May God bless all your footsteps.

Your friend, J.P.

Dear Brett and Eveline,

I'm hoping we will have connected by phone by the time you read this, but please be assured of our prayers and supplications for you both, as well as for Abbi, Stefanie, Katie, and Blake. We are so very sorry you have to go through this—we know you've had some significant trials and upheavals the last couple of years. We'll be praying that the Lord will fill your hearts and home with calm and courage and His perfect peace. We'll be praying for your doctors as well. I know you'll have many, many people lifting you up to Him.

In Christ, Jamie and Orel Hershiser

Dear Brett & Eveline:

How devastated we were to learn of your news last night. You will be in our prayers constantly, and I hope the love and support of so many people who love you will be a great comfort to you during this time. You both are such special people that have such great witness to so many. If anyone can beat this, Brett Butler can and will! May God's love and grace fill you daily.

L. and B.

Dear Mr. Butler:

I wish there was some way I could help you heal, take away the cancer, put things back to normal for you, your family, and your colleagues. It may sound silly for a stranger to feel that way, but I've been watching you play for years and I feel like you're a member of my family. It's been a whole range of emotions for me. I was saddened about the loss of your dear mother. I was ecstatic about your return to Los Angeles. I was miffed about the whole strike/replacement player nightmare. And I ached when the Dodgers' playoff hopes were quashed in Cincinnati. All of this pales in comparison to what's going on now.

I've never been very religious, but if all you ask from your fans and colleagues is our prayers, well, how could I not comply? Offering my heartfelt prayers is the least I can do.

Love, S.L.R.

Dear Fred Claire:

Several years ago I was sitting in the Dodger dugout before a game enjoying the pre-game practice when Brett Butler came to sit beside me. We struck up a casual conversation that ranged from my relationship with my cousin Joe DiMaggio to Brett's childhood baseball days. Although I'm sure he doesn't remember the specific conversation, it was nevertheless an enjoyable one for me.

The point for my writing is to respectfully request that this letter be forwarded to Mr. Butler with my best wishes for his recovery from his recent illness and to let him know that the above conversation that we shared meant a great deal to me. In a time when baseball has more than its share of arrogant prima donnas, Brett Butler has consistently been one of the classiest men in the game who is always willing to entertain a youngster's request for an autograph or have a casual talk with a Dodger fan such as myself.

Sincerely, Vince DiMaggio

Dear Brett and Eveline:

You and your family are not walking alone through the valley this summer. We know that the Lord Jesus walks with you. And you will be bathed in prayer by countless friends all over the land. We are praying. We are honored to be among your world of believing friends. We admire you. We love you.

Waddy and Jean Spoelstra
Founder, Baseball Chapel

Dear Mr. Butler,

I'm sure you do not remember what you were doing on Friday, May 27, 1983, but I certainly do. The Atlanta Braves played the Chicago Cubs, and I was an honorary bat girl for the game. And I was thirteen years old. The other players ignored me and went about their business, but you introduced yourself and said it was good to have me there and that you hoped I had fun. I was flabbergasted. That small gesture made quite an impression on me.

I wish you and your family strength and good wishes through this difficult time. Our prayers will be with you. Thank you for touching my life in a small but very significant way.

L.M. (Emory University, Class of '91)

Dear Brett:

Gayle and I heard that you were recently diagnosed with throat cancer and wanted to let you know that you are in our thoughts and prayers. California has rooted for you as a Los Angeles Dodger and as a San Francisco Giant—we'll kindly overlook your years in Atlanta—and you can be assured that fans throughout the state are pulling for you as you face your greatest challenge yet.

Sincerely, Pete Wilson, Governor, State of California

Dear Brett:

Everyone here in New York was saddened to hear about your diagnosis. We know the fighter that Brett Butler is as a player and as a person. We know you will triumph over this setback in your life. Everyone sends their best wishes to you and your family through this difficult period. Hope to see you when we are in Los Angeles. Our prayers are with you at all times.

Joe McIlvaine and the staff of the New York Mets

Dear Mr. Butler:

I'm not even going to lie to you and say I'm a big Dodger fan, because I'm not. In fact, I despise anything related to Dodger blue. However, there has always been one exception: a certain ball player named Brett Butler.

I was only 4'9" tall until my sophomore year of high school, but during this time I became fascinated with one Brett Butler who also wasn't very tall but yet always worked hard, played hard, and never took his skills for granted. I used you as my role model and began to teach myself how to play at the grand height of 5'6". I finally made the baseball team my senior year of high school. When I heard about your cancer, I was shocked and worried. I have all the faith in the world that you'll beat this. God speed and good luck. Keep the faith.

R.M.

Dear Brett:

We need you in baseball! We need more like you! So I and many others will be praying for your 100% recovery and a speedy return to the game we love. Hang in there! The Lord will be with you!

Your brother in Christ, J.R.

Brett,

You are in our prayers. You will beat this thing.

John and Rose Franco

Dear Brett:

Since I started coaching, you have been the example I use with my Little Leaguers. I have always told them you don't have to be big to be a good player, and you don't have to be big to be a leader. You don't have to be big to be a good sport or a gentleman, and most of all, you don't have to be big to have heart.

Today at practice, I told them all that you are not well, and that I was going to write you and have them all sign the letter. At tomorrow's game we are making you our honorary team captain. We hope this letter makes you feel a little better and we wish you a speedy recovery.

Signed by the coach and the entire team

Dear Mr. Butler:

As a Cincinnati Reds fan for over forty years, and as a follower of Jesus Christ for twenty-five years, I have long wished for the deal that would finally make you a Cincinnati Red. I have appreciated your abilities on the field for a long time, but I have appreciated far more your stand for Christ and the positive values you have brought to baseball. I join the many thousands of fellow believers who are praying for God's healing power to be poured upon you until the cancer is completely gone.

Yours and His, B.D.

Dear Brett,

I am a teacher, and when the news came out of your illness, it was the topic of talk in my classroom. I wanted you to know how many of my high school students respected and admired you. You are the favorite of so many teams, and as an educator I truly commend you for being a role model. You have been immortalized through your positive attitude and great playing.

A.G.

Dear Mr. Butler:

I have no idea why fine young Christians suffer: I only know that God in His infinite wisdom has a purpose for your life. I realize how easy it is for me to say that, as I sit here in perfect health, but I know that it is the right thing to say, nevertheless.

I pledge to you that I shall pray each and every day for you to have the peace that passes human understanding, the courage to endure the pain, and the faith that your life and the lives of your loved ones are in the hands of an all-knowing and loving and merciful God. I will pray for your children and your wife that they will be strong and supportive. I will pray that God will allow you to experience His mercy and His grace.

K.P.

Dear Mr. Butler:

On May 21, 1996, I woke up to my 90th birthday but also to the fact that you were in surgery at the time. It was a time of celebration for me but also for much prayer for you during the day. Yes, I believe in miracles. I had serious cancer surgery in 1967, but with much prayer and care here I am some thirty years later feeling fine.

God bless you and your family, and my prayers will be with you.

M.C.

Dear Brett:

You have meant so much to baseball, to the life of those around you, and those for whom you set an example.

I'll rue forever the deal that sent you away—the worst—and wish that you could have shared the recent success of the Braves. But this is vain, considering the battle you now face. God speed. May the Lord bless you and keep you.

Furman Bisher, Sports Editor, Atlanta Journal

Hi Brett,

You are in for some rough days ahead, but God will see you through. Keep your spirits up and believe with all your heart that you will beat this. It is only human nature to question why, but God has a plan for your life. God be with you and your family. Stand on His promises and never take your eyes off the cross.

J.R.

Dear Brett:

As you may know, I have just come through a very intense encounter with cancer. At a regular checkup I discovered that I had non-Hodgkin's lymphoma. After two surgeries and six chemotherapy treatments, I am now in remission. I have so much to be thankful for just to be able to say that word—remission! I have no guarantees, but then again neither does anyone else. In a very real sense, I do know what you are going through.

We are praying for your wife and children. God is faithful!

David Jeremiah
Pastor and radio preacher

Brett,

When my kids ask me why I have your baseball card on my wall, I tell them the Brett Butler story and how your accomplishments have inspired me daily to reach a little higher than my grasp. Get well and get back on the field.

T.G.

Dear Brett:

Our weakness is a stage on which God's power is enacted before the eyes of the world. May He continue to bless and keep you. I know He will. Blessings to Eveline and the children.

L.F.

Dear Brett:

I want to take this opportunity to express my sincere thanks to you for all that you did for me, both as a player and as a friend.

Brett, your loyalty, hard work, and dedication will forever be appreciated. I was honored to have you play for me. You know how much I loved you and your family. Tell Eveline, Abbi, Stefanie, Katie, and the incomparable Blake that I will love them until the day I die.

Brett, you will always be a credit to your God, your family, and the great game of baseball.

I hope that 1997 will be a healthy, happy, and successful year for you and your family. I really miss being with you. May God bless you and your wonderful family.

Your ex-skipper and friend, Tom Lasorda

Dear Brett:

I have followed your career since the first minor league stats we could get from the sporting news when you were in Richmond. As a Libertyville native, it has always been fun to brag that you know a major-leaguer.

My family and I will be praying for you and yours.

Also, let me thank you. After being a seriously addicted tobacco chewer for the last thirteen years, your story has hit too close to the heart. I don't know if anyone can pin down an exact reason why or how life-threatening disease exists or strikes, but sometimes out of one person's challenges another gets the kick in the rear that he needs. I have quit and have been off the stuff for more than a week.

S.L.

Dear Brett and Eveline:

Just a note to tell you that we are in constant prayer on your behalf. Please know how very special you and your precious children are to me. I know that prayers are answered. Be strong and know that you have lots of people praying for you.

B.C.

Brett,

Sure are praying for you. We have a strong prayer group here in Franklin, Tennessee. Stay strong! If there's anything else I can do for you, please let me know. May the Lord continue to draw us all closer to Him in an awesome way.

Your friend, Michael W. Smith
Christian recording artist

Eveline,

I saw this and God nudged me to get it for you. I think he thought you needed to know how special you are to others and to Him. I really believe God hugs us through others. We love you now and always.

Dyan, John, Andrew, and Rachel Smoltz
Dyan Smoltz is a friend of Eveline's. With this card came a gold ring Eveline has worn every day since as a reminder of God's love.

Dear Brett:

My mother is battling cancer as we speak, and I can only tell you that the one thing more powerful than a deadly disease is love. We have lots of faith. And so do you.

Brett, I always wanted to tell you how special an athlete you are. I wanted to tell you during the strike when you stood by your guns in an unfriendly and unsympathetic environment. I wanted to tell you when you made my little boy feel special on the field before a game. I wanted to tell you when I watched you tough out an at bat last year to beat the Phillies in the ninth. But now, more than ever, I want to tell you that you have what you need to beat this thing. Guts, hope, love, faith, and will.

We all love you Brett. Get well soon.

Roy Firestone and family

Brett:

I know nothing I can say or do can help the pain the frustration you must be feeling, but I did want you to know my thoughts and my prayers are with you. It's obviously a scary time for you and your family, but you have always been a fighter and your faith in God plus your faith in your family and friends will help you battle anything life subjects you to.

Again, my prayers for you and your family. Keep the faith.

Sincerely, Dallas Green
New York Mets

Bugsy,

I'm hurting right now for you and your wife. I really don't know what to pray for either. It was tough and very shocking news. Lack of understanding of God is very uncomfortable for me. It seems at the times you need to understand Him the most you don't. When I heard the news I wanted answers, as you can imagine, and felt empty. It hurts.

Your wife is especially in my thoughts. She is great! The Lord bless and take care of her and you.

B.B.

Bugsy,

You know God wouldn't put anything on your shoulders you couldn't handle. I will be praying and thinking about you. Hang in there pal. Be tough for all of us. Remember, you're Brett Butler.

Darren Hall

Dear Mr. Butler:

I just wanted to write you a note to let you know that my whole family is praying for you during this time. You have been such a tremendous example in your Christian walk and have inspired so many.

I know the Lord will remain faithful to you too—as He always is. Stay strong in the Lord. We serve a mighty God. And remember, nothing is too difficult for Him. We'll continue to pray for healing for you and strength for you and your family.

J.B.

Dear Brett:

I know you probably don't remember, but a couple of years ago during spring training a group of our Little Leaguers spent a day at Dodger town during which they had a chance to mingle and talk to your teammates. Your recent illness certainly had an impact on many that are now playing senior and junior ball, because many have taken to heart your advice concerning tobacco usage. More than any other player at that spring training, you took the time to talk to them the most and they came to identify with you as a ball player.

I hope this finds you and yours well and all is going good for you. I, along with all the members of our league, wish you a speedy recovery. We'll be looking for you back on the diamond.

R.B.

APPENDIX II

BRETT BUTLER

Height: 5-10
Bats: Left
Opening Day Age: 39
Birthplace: Los Angeles, California

Weight: 161
Throws: Left
Birth Date: June 15, 1957

CAREER FIELDING STATISTICS

YR	TEAM	G	PO	A	E	TC	DP	FPct
1981	Atlanta	37	76	2	1	79	0	.987
1982	Atlanta	77	129	2	0	131	0	1.000
1983	Atlanta	143	284	13	4	301	4	.987
1984	Cleveland	156	448	13	4	465	3	.991
1985	Cleveland	150	437	19	1	457	5	.998
1986	Cleveland	159	434	9	3	446	3	.993
1987	Cleveland	136	393	4	4	401	2	.990
1988	San Francisco	155	395	3	5	403	1	.988
1989	San Francisco	152	407	11	6	424	3	.986
1990	San Francisco	159	420	4	6	430	0	.986
1991	Los Angeles	161	372	8	0	380	3	1.000
1992	Los Angeles	155	353	9	2	364	3	.995
1993	Los Angeles	155	369	6	0	375	0	1.000
1994	Los Angeles	111	260	8	2	270	2	.993
1995	N.Y./L.A.	129	282	6	1	290	1	.995
1996	Los Angeles	34	74	1	1	76	0	.987
1997*	Los Angeles	34	69	2	0	71	1	1.000
TOTALS		**2103**	**5202**	**120**	**41**	**5363**	**31**	**.992**

(G=Games, PO=Put Outs, A=Assists, E=Errors, TC=Total Chances, DP=Double Plays, FPct.=Fielding Percentage)
* Statistics as of June 15, 1997

CAREER BATTING STATISTICS

YR	TEAM	G	AB	R	H	2B	3B	HR	RBI	BB	AVG	SO	SB
1979	Bradenton	30	111	36	41	7	5	3	20	19	.369	15	5
	Greenwood	35	117	25	37	2	4	1	11	24	.318	27	20
1980	Anderson	70	255	73	76	12	6	1	26	67	.298	29	44
	Durham	66	224	47	82	15	6	2	39	67	.365	30	36
1981	Richmond	125	466	83	156	19	4	3	36	103	.335	63	44
	ATLANTA	40	126	17	32	2	3	0	4	19	.254	17	9
1982	Richmond	41	157	22	57	8	3	1	22	22	.363	19	12
	ATLANTA	89	240	35	52	2	0	0	7	25	.217	35	21
1983	ATLANTA	151	549	84	154	21	13	5	37	54	.281	56	39
1984	CLEVELAND	159	602	108	162	25	9	3	49	86	.269	62	52
1985	CLEVELAND	152	591	106	184	28	14	5	50	63	.311	42	47
1986	CLEVELAND	161	587	92	163	17	14	4	51	70	.278	65	32
1987	CLEVELAND	137	522	91	154	25	8	9	41	91	.295	55	33
1988	SAN FRANCISCO	157	568	109	163	27	9	6	43	97	.287	64	43
1989	SAN FRANCISCO	154	594	100	168	22	4	4	36	59	.283	69	31
1990	SAN FRANCISCO	160	622	108	192	20	9	3	44	90	.309	62	51
1991	LOS ANGELES	161	615	112	182	13	5	2	38	108	.296	79	38
1992	LOS ANGELES	157	553	86	171	14	11	3	39	95	.309	67	41
1993	LOS ANGELES	156	607	80	181	21	10	1	42	86	.298	69	39
1994	LOS ANGELES	111	417	79	131	13	9	8	33	68	.314	52	27
1995	NEW YORK (NL)	90	367	54	114	13	7	1	25	43	.311	42	21
	LOS ANGELES	39	146	24	40	5	2	0	13	24	.274	9	11
1996	LOS ANGELES	34	131	22	35	1	1	0	8	9	.267	22	8
1997*	LOS ANGELES	37	131	18	42	4	1	0	6	24	.321	11	4
NL TOTALS		**1536**	**5666**	**928**	**1657**	**178**	**84**	**33**	**375**	**801**	**.292**	**654**	**383**
AL TOTALS		**609**	**2302**	**397**	**663**	**95**	**45**	**21**	**191**	**310**	**.288**	**224**	**164**
TOTALS		**2145**	**7968**	**1325**	**2320**	**273**	**129**	**54**	**566**	**1111**	**.289**	**878**	**547**

(G=Games, AB=At Bats, R=Runs, H=Hits, 2B=doubles, 3B=triples, HR=Home Runs, RBI=Runs Batted In, BB=Base on Balls, Avg.=Batting Average, SO=Strike Outs, SB=Stolen Bases)
* Statistics as of June 15, 1997

CAREER TRANSACTIONS

- Selected by Atlanta Braves in the twenty-third round of the June 1979 Free Agent Draft.
- Traded with Brook Jacoby to Cleveland Indians on October 21, 1983, completing deal in which Atlanta acquired pitcher Len Barker for three players to be named later on August 28, 1983. Cleveland acquired pitcher Rick Behenna as partial completion of deal on September 2, 1983.
- Signed by San Francisco Giants as a free agent on December 1, 1987.
- Signed by Los Angeles Dodgers as a free agent on December 15, 1990.
- Signed by New York Mets as a free agent on April 11, 1995.
- Traded to Los Angeles from the New York Mets for outfielders Dwight Maness and Scott Hunter on August 18, 1995.

CAREER AND GAME HIGHS

Most Hits: 5 (five times), last time April 16, 1997, at New York.

Most Runs: 4 (two times), last time April 12, 1990, at Atlanta (with San Francisco).

Most RBI: 4 (two times), last time August 8, 1985, at New York (with Cleveland).

Most HR: 2, August 8, 1985, at New York (with Cleveland).

Longest Hitting Streak: 23 games, June 15-July 12, 1991.

Most Stolen Bases: 3 (five times), last time July 25, 1992, at Montreal.

Career Grand Slams: 1, September 14, 1984, at Oakland (with Cleveland).

1996 NOTES

- Finished the season with a .267 average (35-for-131), 22 runs, 1 double, 1 triple, 8 RBI, and 8 stolen bases.
- Named the 1996 recipient of the fifth annual Branch Rickey Award, given annually to Major League Baseball's outstanding individual who personifies "service above self" . . . also received the Vincent Lombardi Award in recognition of outstanding accomplishments in the sports world, dedication to community, and strong commitment to inner-city youth.
- He is one of only 26 major leaguers in history to collect 2,000 base hits and 500 stolen bases.
- Was voted the best bunter in the majors by major league managers for *Baseball America's* "Tools of the Trade."
- Named the Most Inspirational Player by the local Southern California Chapter of the Baseball Writers Association of America.
- Began the season with a five-game hitting streak, batting .286 (6-for-21), with 3 runs, and stolen base.
- Collected a season-high 4 hits on April 20 at Florida . . . had 5 total multiple-hit games.
- Had just one multiple-RBI game, collecting two on April 14 vs. Florida.
- Hit in a season-high six-straight games from April 20-25 and was 9-for-24 (.375) with 6 runs, a double, triple, and 2 RBI . . . also hit in six-straight games from April 28-May 1 and September 6-7, when he went 7-for-25 (.280) with four runs and 1 RBI.
- Had only 1 bunt hit in 1996, bringing his career total to 281.

- Collected seven infield hits, bringing his total to 215 with the Dodgers.
- Went 19 straight at-bats without striking out, April 23-28.
- He led off in 15 games and batted .231 (12-for-52) with 10 runs and 5 walks.
- Scored the game-winning run on September 6 vs. Pittsburgh, his first game back, when Eric Karros hit a sacrifice fly in the eighth inning.
- Started the Dodgers first 29 games and batted .265 with a double, triple, 7 RBI, and 7 stolen bases.
- Placed on the DL on May 2 when he went to Atlanta for a tonsillectomy . . . on May 6, a cancerous plum-size tumor was discovered in his tonsils . . . the cancer is known as squamous cell carcinoma . . . had surgery to remove the tumor and lymph nodes on May 21 at Emory University . . . surgery was performed by Dr. William Grist . . . began radiation treatment on June 17, which lasted six weeks and two days (thirty-two treatments).
- Had previously been placed on the disabled list only once in his career in 1987 with the Indians when he fractured the middle finger on his left hand attempting to bunt on Opening Day and missed the entire month of April.
- Rejoined the team on August 26 in Montreal and was reinstated from the DL on September 6.
- Played in just five games after returning, batting .286 (4-for-14) with 4 runs scored and 1 RBI.
- Hit on the left hand with a pitch while attempting to bunt in the fourth inning on September 10 . . . suffered a fractured fifth metacarpal in his left hand and missed the remainder of the 1996 season.
- His .992 lifetime fielding average is second all-time among outfielders behind Terry Puhl's .993 mark . . . committed only 1 error in 1996 and has made just 41 errors in 5,363 total chances during his career.

- Had only eight stolen bases in 1996 because of his limited playing time, marking the first time in his major-league career he did not record 20 or more thefts . . . stole 30 or more bases on 12 occasions.
- Entering the 1997 season, Butler among active players ranked first in triples (128), fourth in stolen bases (543), sixth in walks (1,087), seventh in runs (1,307), ninth in hits (2,278), tenth in games played (2,108) and twenty-fifth in on-base percentage (.377).